Remote Teaching and Learning in the Elementary ELA Classroom

Teaching in remote, distance, and hybrid environments can be overwhelming and confusing and poses many challenges for novice and veteran teachers alike. In this comprehensive and practice-ready book, you'll find clear ideas for implementing the best practices of English-language instruction in remote teaching settings. Understanding that remote teaching looks different in each subject, Ruday and Jacobson identify methods specifically designed for elementary English language arts classrooms.

Designed for use in remote, hybrid, and hyflex environments with synchronous or asynchronous learning, this resource gives teachers a toolbox of research-backed recommendations, ideas, examples, and practices for teaching in unpredictable and new environments. Ruday and Jacobson address essential topics, including writing, grammar, and reading instruction; assessment; differentiation; culturally relevant teaching; family engagement and communication; technology; professional self-care; and more. Teachers will come away with ready-to-implement strategies and insights for high-quality instruction that can be adapted to any kind of remote learning environment.

Sean Ruday is an associate professor of English education at Longwood University and a former classroom teacher. He frequently writes and presents on innovative ways to improve students' literacy learning. You can follow him on Twitter at @SeanRuday and visit his website at www.seanruday. weebly.com.

Taylor M. Jacobson is a fifth-grade teacher at Glenwood Elementary, Virginia. You can follow her on Twitter at @mstjacobson.

Other Eye on Education Books
Available from Routledge
(www.routledge.com/eyeoneducation)

The Elementary School Grammar Toolkit, Second Edition Using Mentor Texts to Teach Standards-Based Language and Grammar in Grades 3–5
Sean Ruday

The Middle School Grammar Toolkit, Second Edition Using Mentor Texts to Teach Standards-Based Language and Grammar in Grades 6–8
Sean Ruday

Inquiry-Based Literature Instruction in the 6–12 Classroom: A Hands-on Guide for Deeper Learning
Sean Ruday and Katie Caprino

The Multimedia Writing Toolkit Helping Students Incorporate Graphics and Videos for Authentic Purposes, Grades 3–8
Sean Ruday

The Informational Writing Toolkit Using Mentor Texts in Grades 3–5
Sean Ruday

The Argument Writing Toolkit Using Mentor Texts in Grades 6–8
Sean Ruday

The Narrative Writing Toolkit Using Mentor Texts in Grades 3–8
Sean Ruday

The First-Year English Teacher's Guidebook Strategies for Success
Sean Ruday

Culturally Relevant Teaching in the English Language Arts Classroom
Sean Ruday

Rigor in the Remote Learning Classroom Instructional Tips and Strategies
Barbara R. Blackburn

Thriving as an Online K-12 Educator Essential Practices from the Field Jody Peerless Green From Texting to Teaching Grammar Instruction in a Digital Age
Jeremy Hyler and Troy Hicks

Remote Teaching and Learning in the Elementary ELA Classroom

Instructional Strategies and Best Practices

Sean Ruday and Taylor M. Jacobson

Routledge
Taylor & Francis Group

NEW YORK AND LONDON

First published 2021
by Routledge
605 Third Avenue, New York, NY 10158

and by Routledge
2 Park Square, Milton Park, Abingdon, Oxon, OX14 4RN

Routledge is an imprint of the Taylor & Francis Group, an informa business

Library of Congress Cataloging-in-Publication Data
A catalog record for this book has been requested

ISBN: 978-0-367-74165-5 (hbk)
ISBN: 978-0-367-72389-7 (pbk)
ISBN: 978-1-003-15635-2 (ebk)

Typeset in Palatino
by Apex CoVantage, LLC

Access the Support Material: routledge.com/9780367723897

Contents

Meet the Authors

Sean Ruday is an associate professor and program coordinator of English education at Longwood University and a former classroom teacher. He began his teaching career at a public school in Brooklyn, New York, and has taught English and language arts at public and private schools in New York, Massachusetts, and Virginia. He holds a BA from Boston College, an MA from New York University, and a PhD from the University of Virginia. Some publications in which his works have appeared are *Issues in Teacher Education*, *Journal of Teaching Writing*, *Journal of Language and Literacy Education*, and *Contemporary Issues in Technology and Teacher Education*. Sean frequently writes and presents on innovative ways to improve students' literacy learning. You can follow Sean on Twitter at @SeanRuday and visit his website at www.seanruday. weebly.com.

Taylor M. Jacobson is a fifth-grade teacher at Glenwood Elementary in Virginia Beach, Virginia. She began her journey into education in high school at Tallwood High School's Virginia Teachers for Tomorrow program in 2013. She holds a BA from Longwood University and is currently pursuing her MEd from Old Dominion University. She has been published in the *Virginia English Journal* for her work on social justice education in the classroom and is committed to learning more about representative literature and culturally responsive education. You can follow Taylor's classroom escapades on Twitter at @mstjacobson.

Acknowledgments

Sean's Acknowledgments

I want to thank everyone at Routledge Eye on Education—especially amazing editor Karen Adler—for the insight, guidance, and support.

I would like to thank my parents, Bob and Joyce Ruday. I am grateful for their encouragement in all aspects of my life.

Finally, I want to thank my wife, Clare Ruday. I can't imagine my life without the happiness she brings to it.

Taylor's Acknowledgments

I want to, foremost, thank Sean Ruday for seeing something I never saw in myself and always keeping me in mind when his brain wheels start turning. And thank you to Routledge Eye on Education for allowing us to share this work with the world.

I want to thank my coworkers, especially Danielle Ganze, Nancy Munson, and Melissa Fano, for their guidance, humor, support, and your love for education.

I would like to thank Jenna Free, my Virginia Teachers for Tomorrow teacher from high school. She was one of the first people who ever believed in my skill as a teacher vocally, and the confidence she had in me was the spark of the successful career I am pursuing today.

I want to thank my mema, Kay Fleetwood, for calling me an "immature writer" when I wrote my college entrance essay: that inspired me to be the author I am today but, more than that, for being a phone call away when I can't remember the word I'm looking for or when I forget how important the work I do is.

Finally, I want to thank my partner, Paul Kastorff, who has always supported the work I do as a teacher and, of course, for bringing me coffee when I was busy writing.

Support Material

Many of the tools discussed and displayed in this book are also available on the Routledge website as Adobe Acrobat files. Permission has been granted to purchasers of this book to download these tools and print them. You can access these downloads by visiting www.routledge.com/9780367723897. Then click on the tab that says "Support Material" and select the files. They will begin downloading to your computer.

Introduction

Visions and Decisions in a New Educational Environment

For us, the new educational environment of remote and distance learning has led to a great deal of reflection—and, since you're reading this book, we suspect it may have done the same for you. As we've thought about our work with our students (Taylor with her elementary schoolers and Sean with the preservice teachers he mentors and the elementary school literacy classes with which he works), we've considered what language arts instruction should look like in the many forms of remote and distance learning. We've asked ourselves questions such as:

- How can remote elementary school language arts instruction incorporate research-based best instructional practices?
- How can teachers and students build effective and supportive remote learning communities?
- How can remote language arts instruction foster meaningful class discussions and student collaboration?
- How can we as teachers work for equitable educational opportunities for our students in the remote learning context?
- How can we incorporate culturally relevant and sustaining instructional practices in remote language arts instruction?
- What are some especially important ideas to consider regarding the many instructional technological resources being promoted?
- What are the best ways for teachers to communicate with and support students' caregivers?
- How can teachers be sure to take care of themselves in this new and challenging time?

These questions, and others like them, form the fundamental basis of this book, which we've designed to provide elementary school language arts teachers with a practical and comprehensive resource that describes how to implement the best practices of language arts instruction in today's world of remote instruction and beyond. We say "beyond" because the ideas and strategies discussed in this book are relevant not only during the time schools are moved online due to COVID-19 but also in the future when administrators, teachers, and students can think about what instructional practices incorporated during this time may be useful to further enhance language arts instruction.

We decided to write this book to provide teachers with a thorough, research-based, and practice-ready book that conveys clear ideas about effective elementary school language arts instruction and describes specific ways to put those ideas into action in the various distance learning settings in which today's educators find themselves while also giving them the tools and insights to think about ways they might continue to utilize some of these practices. As the authors of this book, we have two main complementary goals. The first is to help teachers think about and identify the best methods of elementary grades language arts instruction, such as culturally relevant teaching, inquiry-based learning, mentor text use, writing instruction, and student collaboration. The second is to provide teachers with concrete recommendations, ideas, and examples to help them put these best-practice strategies into action in their remote teaching practice. Since there are a variety of ways that educational practices in today's world can look, such as completely online, hybrid learning, and hyflex constructions, we discuss how the book's instructional insights can be adapted for this range of formats. We want teachers to finish reading this book and think, "I know about high-quality language arts instruction, *and* I know how to implement it in remote learning!"

Effective Remote Language Arts Instruction

It's so easy for teachers to be overwhelmed with all of the technological tools, apps, and programs that are often brought up in conversations about remote learning. Because of these many options and innovations, teachers may feel anxious due to a lack of familiarity with some programs and pressure to utilize them without understanding what they are. While many technological tools can positively impact teaching and learning, we encourage teachers to think carefully about these resources and reflect on their potential usefulness before utilizing them in remote instruction. An especially effective way to do this is to consider whether specific technological tools, resources, and programs align with their pedagogical goals and are effective ways of achieving those goals (Ruday, 2016; Young & Bush, 2004). Instead of starting with a resource, app, or program and making instruction align with its features, we encourage language arts teachers to decide on their instructional objectives and then select tools that are the best ways to fit that objective.

We believe that the best remote language arts instruction is not rooted in a specific app, program, or website but instead in thoughtful decision-making that carefully considers the relevant learning goals and student needs and uses that information to identify the best ways to help students learn. Teachers will certainly need to consider their available resources and instructional contexts in this decision-making process, but we feel that the best remote instruction is the kind that maximizes student learning and uses available programs as vehicles for that learning. For example, if we language teachers want to hold one-on-one writing conferences with our students, we should select resources and programs that facilitate this type of interaction. Similarly, if our objective is to engage students in inquiry-based learning that gives them opportunities to create and investigate questions that matter to them, we would identify and use tools that align with this instructional practice. By being intentional with the instructional resources we use, we can engage our students in remote language arts instruction that maximizes their learning.

We've subtitled this introduction "Visions and Decisions in a New Educational Environment" because of the importance we place on aligning our beliefs about effective instructions with specific practices. Whether we teach in an in-person, remote, hybrid, or hyflex model, it's essential that we make decisions about teaching and learning that correspond with our beliefs about the best practices of elementary school language arts instruction. For instance, if one of our core beliefs about strong grammar instruction is that grammatical concepts are taught in the context of effective writing using mentor texts, we can make instructional decisions that put this idea into action in ways that align with the instructional modality we're using. If we believe that it's essential to provide students with opportunities to build background knowledge of topics they read about and make meaningful connections while reading, let's ensure that our instructional practices and decisions correspond with that vision.

While schools were forced into remote learning in 2020 due to the COVID-19 pandemic, it's important to note that the educational practices utilized during this time can continue to be relevant and useful even when schools return to fully in-person instruction. If some of the instructional practices utilized during remote and distance learning prove to be the best ways for us language arts teachers to help students engage with the curriculum, we should continue to implement those practices in some form. For example, if a tool that a teacher utilizes during remote learning facilitates meaningful and effective student collaboration, that teacher can certainly look for ways to continue to make use of that tool in the future, regardless of whether the instruction is delivered entirely remotely or not. Similarly, if a teacher finds that some remote learning components lend themselves to culturally relevant teaching, they can continue to utilize those practices and components in the future because they align with that teacher's instructional beliefs and maximize students' abilities to engage with the curriculum. Now that we've shared key aspects of our beliefs about effective elementary school language arts instruction, let's look at what's in store in this book.

What to Expect in This Book

This book is divided into four sections that we believe work together to provide teachers with the information they need to implement high-quality language arts instruction in a remote elementary-grade context. Section One, "The New 'Classroom,'" contains two chapters that address important ideas for teachers to consider as they create effective, organized, and interactive learning environments. Chapter One, "Building a Learning Community and Supporting Student Behavior in Remote Instruction," provides examples and suggestions to help teachers construct cohesive communities among their students that support effective behavior while navigating the realities of remote and distance learning. These insights are designed to foster learning environments in which students feel comfortable, prepared, and ready to engage in learning—even if they are not in the physical classroom. Chapter Two, "Class Discussion and Student Collaboration in a New Era," provides a logical extension for the ideas in Chapter One: once students feel comfortable in their learning communities, they can effectively work together and share ideas. This chapter describes ways for teachers to facilitate meaningful discussions and to construct collaborative activities, both of which will maximize student learning and help them feel part of a cohesive learning community. After you read this section, we want you to be able to build an educational environment in which students feel comfortable and well supported while engaging them in collaboration that facilitates their learning and their sense of community.

The book's second section, titled "The Potential of Remote Language Arts Instruction," discusses specific instructional tactics that represent the best practices of elementary school language arts teaching and can be effectively adapted to remote contexts. The five chapters in this section detail important components of language arts instruction and discuss ways teachers can implement them in a variety of distance and remote learning situations. Chapter Three, "A New Format of Writing and Grammar Instruction," discusses how the best methods of teaching writing strategies and grammatical concepts, such as mentor text use, writing conferences, and writing workshops, can be effectively utilized when students are learning remotely. Chapter Four, "Reading Instruction in the Remote Environment," provides insights into ways we language arts teachers can help our students have effective and engaging reading experiences while utilizing features and attributes of remote learning.

In Chapter Five, "Culturally Relevant and Sustaining Teaching and Learning in Remote Contexts," we discuss how teachers can incorporate the principles of culturally relevant and culturally sustaining pedagogy in remote elementary school language arts instruction, discussing key components of culturally relevant and sustaining teaching and describing ways that remote instruction can be used to facilitate this important instructional strategy. Similarly, in Chapter Six, "The Role of Inquiry in Remote Teaching and Learning," we describe ways for teachers to utilize inquiry-based language arts instruction in the remote learning context, sharing important aspects of this instructional approach and discussing the ways it can be effectively incorporated in remote teaching and learning. This section concludes with Chapter Seven, "Assessing Student Learning"; in this chapter, we describe important assessment-related ideas to guide you as you utilize effective formative and summative assessments in the context of remote language arts instruction. The ideas and methods discussed in this section align with the book's goal of ensuring that readers understand the key components of effective elementary school language arts instruction and the best ways to put them into practice in remote instruction.

The third section of the book, "Teacher Roles in a New World," contains three chapters designed to guide and support teachers as they navigate the unique challenges of the remote learning environment. Chapter Eight, "Communicating With and Supporting Students' Caregivers," addresses one such aspect of the new educational world, describing tactics educators can use to most effectively communicate with and support our students' caregivers in the context of remote teaching and learning. In Chapter Nine, "Reflecting on Technology," we provide insights and recommendations for teachers to use to make the technology used in their remote instruction strategic and equitable. As we discuss in more depth in Chapter Nine, remote learning has highlighted important issues related to instructional technology, such as the importance of aligning technological tools with specific learning goals and being mindful of issues related to technology access. This section concludes with Chapter Ten, "Taking Care of Yourself," which discusses self-care ideas that are especially relevant to teachers navigating the professional and personal challenges associated with the demands of remote teaching. This chapter describes ways to create work–life balance and manage stress, ensuring that educators take care of themselves so they can best help their students. After reading these three chapters, educators will have additional tools at their disposal for succeeding in a changed reality.

The book concludes with Section Four, which features information and resources designed to help you put the ideas in this book into action. Chapter Eleven, "Key Takeaway Ideas," describes important insights and recommendations to facilitate effective remote teaching and learning experiences for you and your students. Following that, you'll find the book's References section, which cites important sources that you can examine to further develop your understandings of effective remote language arts instruction. Appendix A contains forms, templates, and graphic organizers that you can use when planning your instruction; these resources are designed to help you put the ideas and concepts discussed in this book into action as easily as possible. Finally, the "Guide for Book Studies" in Appendix B identifies thought-provoking reflection questions and prompts to consider when using this book as a book-study text. We highly recommend engaging in a book study of this text with other teachers in your professional learning network; doing so can allow you to collaboratively discuss the ideas and practices the book describes and brainstorm ways to apply its ideas to your own instruction.

For consistency and ease of use, each chapter in this book that describes an educational strategy follows a similar pattern: we discuss the chapter's focal topic, explain how it aligns with remote learning, share an example from Taylor's work as an elementary school language arts teacher, provide teachers with key recommendations to consider when implementing the focal topic in their own practice, and discuss how the chapter's concept can be utilized in a wide range of instructional modalities, including entirely remote instruction (in which instruction is completely virtual), hybrid instruction (in which students are physically present in the classroom some days and engage through virtual learning other days), and hyflex instruction (in which some students are physically present in the classroom and other students join at the same time virtually). As you read this book, you'll engage with many ideas about the best practices of elementary school language arts instruction and with clear and concrete suggestions for enacting them in the context of remote learning. While many of us entered into remote learning because of

COVID-19, we, as the authors of this book, see the suggestions described in this text as having relevance beyond the pandemic. We believe that the educational innovations and remote learning tactics first employed out of necessity have the potential to have lasting impacts on education by taking advantage of technological resources, innovative practices, and 21st-century communication tools. This book will guide you as you consider research-based best practices of language arts instruction, reflect on ways to implement those practices in remote learning, and envision future instruction that draws from the most useful aspects of educational innovations. So if you're ready to learn more about strong elementary school language arts teaching and learning in remote contexts, keep reading!

1

The New "Classroom"

1

Building a Learning Community and Supporting Student Behavior in Remote Instruction

In this chapter, we explore the concept of constructing a strong learning community and supporting student behavior in remote instruction, which is both a significant challenge and a key aspect of instructional learning success. The information in this chapter provides important information about the features and significance of such a community and conveys useful suggestions to consider when building a strong sense of connection that supports effective behavior among students during remote instruction. First, we explore what it means to build a learning community that supports student behavior in the time of remote instruction, highlighting attributes, challenges, and opportunities associated with constructing a strong remote learning community. We then reflect on why doing so is especially important, which we follow with an instructional snapshot section that provides an example of Taylor's work with her students. After that, we share key recommendations for teachers to consider when building strong remote learning communities with their students. Finally, we discuss how the ideas described in this chapter can be utilized in and adapted for a wide range of modalities.

What Does It Mean to Build a Learning Community in the Time of Remote Instruction?

Take a minute and think about the term *learning community* and how it relates to effective elementary school language arts instruction. What comes to your mind? It might be a teacher conducting reading and writing mini-lessons with engaged students who are challenged by the content and thinking about ways to apply their newfound knowledge. It could be students working in small groups as they synthesize important ideas from a reading. Perhaps it's students and teachers talking together about how a text, essential question, or concept relates to the contemporary world. It might even be students and teachers smiling and joking together, enjoying the strong sense of community and connection in the classroom. When we (Sean and Taylor) think about the images that "learning community" calls to mind for us, a common theme in those images is the strong relationships that exist: the individuals in the communities we picture are learning, communicating, and interacting in ways that highlight the strong relationships in that community. We love building relationships with our students and helping them feel at home, welcome, and supported in language arts and have developed a variety of tools and tactics to help us do so.

However, the challenge facing us and other educators around the country in the age of remote learning is how we can construct a relationship-driven and supportive learning community in the time of remote instruction. In order to think about how to do this, one early step is to reflect on what the experience of community building in a remote education environment looks like. While certain aspects of learning communities will, of course, differ between instruction that is entirely in person and instruction delivered in remote contexts, we feel there are common components of strong learning communities that exist across learning modalities. Strong learning communities, we believe, do the following:

◆ Prioritize teacher-to-student and student-to-student relationship building.
◆ Center students' individual interests, experiences, and identities.
◆ Use relevance, humor, and genuine connections to create a positive environment that facilitates comfort, learning, and risk-taking.
◆ Feature clear expectations on what it means to be a positive and contributing member of the learning community.

Although some aspects of relationship building can be different in remote learning environments, we believe that it is still possible (and very important) for teachers to work with their students to construct learning communities that foster meaningful relationships and genuine connections in all learning contexts and situations. In the next section, we look in more detail at the importance of strong learning communities that value student relationships.

Why Is This Important?

Research indicates that strong student–teacher relationships can positively impact students' abilities to succeed in school in a variety of ways, such as higher grades, increased engagement, and fewer disruptive behaviors (Quin, 2016). In addition, teachers can help create supportive classroom environments in which students feel safe, are encouraged to collaborate, and are comfortable taking risks (Aspen Institute, 2017). These findings speak to what many teachers and students have noticed through their experiences: strong relationships and learning communities enhance student learning and support effective student behavior. Between the two of us, we've worked with English language arts students in a variety of school settings and have routinely noticed that building community is essential to creating an educational context that facilitates successful teaching and learning.

During the time we've taught in remote contexts, we've identified the importance of community and relationship building when working with students who don't all share the same physical classroom space. We've noticed that virtual contexts can already result in individuals feeling less connected to one another than they might feel in face-to-face settings, so we've made it a priority to be intentional about building communities with our students in order to help students feel comfortable in the learning environment. This feeling of comfort, we've found, not only helps students engage with the course material but also supports them as they follow the established learning and behavior expectations. By building this sense of community, we can help our students achieve the many social and academic benefits that the research cited in this section indicates correspond with a strong learning environment. We strongly believe that constructing a cohesive community is an extremely meaningful aspect of remote and virtual learning. In the next section, we take a look at an example from Taylor's work building community with students in her language arts instruction

Instructional Snapshot: An Example From Taylor's Work

In the first week of school, I read a few books to discuss multiple identities and the importance of acceptance and diversity. The first book we read was *The Day You Begin* by Jaqueline Woodson. This story focuses on stories like language variances, lunch differences, and disparities between summer vacations. Students all have things that are unique about them, but the book discusses that diversity is something to be celebrated. Later that day, I read *Those Shoes* by Maribeth Boelts before wrapping up for the day. That story is about a boy who doesn't have a lot of money and has to go thrift shopping for his shoes. There's a pair he really wants, but the pair they had at the thrift store doesn't fit him. He ends up giving those shoes to another kid in need. Finally, the next day, I read *Just Ask* by Sonia Sotomayor. In this book, the students learned about different disabilities and how you can really just ask if you have questions.

My hope is that all students were able to see something that was a mirror to them, but until I get to know them more, I will need to explore all identities. From all this reading, our class created a "Class Agreements" poster. Some agreements we made were "we will include our classmates" and "we will accept our classmates no matter their differences." Since my class is virtual and has gone from being virtual to in person back to virtual, I have the poster hanging in my room signed, but I also posted it on Schoology, my district's learning management system, as a discussion so all my students could virtually "sign" the agreements as well.

These class agreements are a key part of my classroom community and management. Class agreements put the responsibility to follow them on the students. They have agreed to accept their classmates no matter the differences, so if they are judging another student, I turn them to the class agreements. We can also begin to understand the things that the students consider important in their hearts. What kind of agreements are they recommending? What kind of agreements do they hold dear? So many important parts of the students' values can be exposed in a small activity to build community in the classroom.

Key Recommendations

In this section, we describe key recommendations to keep in mind when building a cohesive and supportive learning community in remote contexts. While doing this in virtual learning situations can be challenging, these suggestions can guide you as a construct an environment in which students and teachers support one another and feel comfortable:

◆ Conduct informal check-ins about noncurricular topics.
◆ Share your own excitement, vulnerability, and personality.
◆ Model what curiosity and learning look like for you.
◆ Center students' identities and experiences in the curriculum.
◆ Create class agreements that prioritize a supportive environment.

By incorporating these recommendations, you'll be building a supportive community that privileges students' ideas and well-being while demonstrating behaviors that contribute to a strong learning environment. Now, let's take a look at each of these suggestions in more detail.

Recommendation One: Conduct Informal Check-Ins About Noncurricular Topics

To build the relationships that are essential to strong learning communities, we recommend having informal check-ins and exchanges with students about noncurricular topics. These interactions can take a wide range of forms, address a number of topics, and be used at a variety of times. For example, you might ask your students a fun "Question of the Day" such as "What song would you listen to on repeat for an hour?" or "If you had to eat one food every day for an entire year, what would it be?" We've also seen teachers ask daily "Would You Rather" questions about a number of engaging topics; this is another enjoyable and informal way to build a classroom community. Before some of his virtual classes, Sean has asked students questions such as "What's something you're excited for this weekend?" and "What's something that has made you happy lately?" We recommend allowing students to choose whether or not they respond to these questions so the interactions have a conversational feel instead of a required one. This naturally fits itself into the Morning Meeting structure from Responsive Classroom. Morning Meeting includes a "sharing" time during which students are encouraged to "share information about important events in their lives. Listeners often offer empathetic comments or ask clarifying questions" (Responsive Classroom, 2016). In many schools, including Taylor's, Morning Meetings are required, so it is best to use these times to really focus on building relationships. In older grades, you may find trouble with students sharing their answers to these questions. Eventually, it can be assumed that those students will become comfortable sharing as the relationships between teacher-to-student and student-to-student develop. While it's possible that still some students may not answer, it's also possible that more students will participate when they feel more comfortable in the learning environment and they learn about one another's interests and ideas.

Although these check-ins can take place before class sessions start, such as a voluntary question that students are invited to answer before a particular class period or during a Morning Meeting, you can conduct them at any time at all that works for you. You might ask check-in with students in the middle of a lesson when you feel their energy might be lagging, or you could devote some end-of-class time to community building by chatting with them about an engaging question or idea towards the end of the instructional period. Regardless of the specific topic of the check-in or the time when it takes place, we encourage you to communicate informally with students about noncurricular topics; doing so can help you construct a close and cohesive community with and among your students.

If you're looking for more of a personal, social-emotional task, Taylor has used an emoji-based system on Schoology. By using Google Slides, she created a slide that students can drag an emoji to show how they're feeling. This can be edited per grade level, for example, giving young students the opportunity to just use the picture, but with students in older grades, you can ask them to write a few short sentences describing why they feel those ways. Through Schoology, her students all create their own copy of this slide, and the only person who can see the slide is the teacher. This helps Taylor see specifically what's bothering her students so that she is prepared to ensure the best environment for her students.

Recommendation Two: Share Your Own Excitement, Vulnerability, and Personality

Another important step toward building a strong classroom community is sharing your own personality traits and discussing things that make you feel excited and vulnerable. Doing this, we feel, can help construct a learning environment that values and embraces authentic feelings: by sharing who we are, we teachers can help create a safe space for students who may be interested in sharing their excitements, vulnerabilities, and personalities. Especially given the uncertainties and challenges in the world, we feel it can be particularly important for us as teachers to construct inclusive and safe classrooms where we model what it looks like to share authentic concerns and interests.

We can share these aspects of our identities in a variety of ways. We can discuss key topics that interest and excite us at the beginning of the school year when introducing ourselves, but this type of authentic expression shouldn't stop there. We can talk with students before and after class about family, music, movies, sports, or anything else that helps our students see us for who we are and what we value. In addition, we can talk with students about how we're feeling about things taking place in our lives that excite us, make us nervous, and convey aspects of our identities.

On the first day of school, Taylor facilitated a "Get to Know Your Teacher" Kahoot. Kahoot is a website that lets students answer questions from their own web-enabled devices. Obviously, the students didn't know much about Taylor yet, but they had received an "About the Teacher" flyer in their goody bags and learned a little through her back-to-school video. The questions allowed her students to get to know her better as she shared a brief Google Slide based on the question asked in the Kahoot. For example, one true-or-false question she gave was "Your teacher is married." Taylor is not married but in a relationship, so she shared about him and the fact that he is deployed with the US Navy. A few hours later, while helping a student with some technology issues, the student's mom pointed out that the student was really excited to hear that Taylor was military-affiliated because the student's father was deployed at the current time.

It's also important to note that, as language arts teachers, our academic subject also facilitates the sharing of personal connections—we can make connections between characters and events in literature and our lives, experiences, and interests. All these conversations and connections are aligned with the structure of remote learning: we can use our virtual learning platforms and spaces to share what matters to us, express our identities, and generally model the process of being open and authentic. By displaying aspects of our identities and selves with our students, we can work toward constructing a learning environment that privileges self-expression.

Recommendation Three: Model What Curiosity and Learning Look Like for You

This recommendation follows logically from the previous one as both address the importance of teachers modeling community-building behaviors. While Recommendation Two calls for us teachers to demonstrate and share authentic aspects of our personalities, this one discusses the process of modeling what curiosity and learning look like for us in our professional and personal lives. Doing this, we feel, can help construct a community that values inquisitive thinking and is excited about learning. Modeling our own curiosities and academic interests can be especially effective in remote learning, where our role as educators can shift a bit to even more of a learning facilitator and less of a traditional instructor who dispenses information. Since students who participate in remote instruction will have some level of access to technological devices, they can find information through these electronic resources. Because of this, it's especially important that we educators create a learning community that prioritizes and values curiosity and the process of learning of one's own interests.

There are a variety of ways to provide this model for students. One tactic that can be especially effective is to routinely discuss your goals as a reader and writer and share your progress in relation to those goals. For example, during a writing workshop, you could discuss a piece of writing you're working on, noting some things you like about it and some ways you think it could be even better. Similarly, you could share reading goals you have, such as hoping to use independent reading time to explore more of the works by a certain author or to delve more deeply into a genre. By modeling these learning goals, you'll work toward building a learning community that values learning goals and will encourage your students to do similar work in their own learning.

Another impactful way to model what curiosity and learning look like for you is to talk with your students about questions you're thinking about and topics you'd like to explore further. These questions and topics can relate to something the class is studying, such as wanting to know more about something discussed in a book the class is reading (such as a time period, event, or another topic relevant to that book), but they can also take other forms. We can share with our students our curiosities about the world, such as authentic questions about human behavior, societal trends, natural phenomena, technology, or anything else that intrigues us. (We discuss the importance of curiosity and asking questions in even more detail in Chapter Six, "The Role of Inquiry in Remote Teaching and Learning.") When we talk with students about what we wonder about, we can help construct a learning community that privileges curiosity and consists of members who share their ideas and wonderings through virtual communication.

Recommendation Four: Center Students' Identities and Experiences in the Curriculum

In order for us teachers to create supportive and inclusive virtual learning communities, it's essential that we use our instruction center students' identities and experiences in the curriculum. By designing learning activities that provide authentic opportunities for students to share their lived experiences and identities, we can build culturally relevant (Ladson-Billings, 1995) and culturally sustaining (Paris, 2012) learning communities that privilege students' cultures and backgrounds and use those attributes to facilitate their learning (Gay, 2002). When we position our students' identities as central to their learning, we communicate an important message to them by showing them we value their unique perspectives and see those components as central to their experiences in school.

A learning community that centers students' identities and experiences in the curriculum can take a number of forms, many of which are explored in even more depth in Chapter Five, "Culturally Relevant and Sustaining Teaching and Learning in Remote Contexts." When building a remote environment that values these components, we encourage you to actively look for opportunities for students to authentically incorporate aspects of their lives in learning activities. For example, if you're talking with students about that writing strategy of using sensory details, you can ask students to find examples of this concept in books, songs, social media posts, and other texts that they encounter in their out-of-school lives. Similarly, if your students are working on word roots, they can identify examples of words they encounter outside of school that contain these roots. In addition, it's important that we allow students to read books that represent them—and to make their own choices about which books represent them—so that they can have opportunities to see themselves in the school curriculum (Bishop, 1990). These instructional practices not only create inclusive learning environments but also can be easily implemented in remote instruction: distance learning is very conducive to student choice, relevance, and agency, as students can select books and other texts that represent them and then share their selections with the class in virtual contexts.

Recommendation Five: Create Class Agreements That Prioritize a Supportive Environment

To help students interact in positive ways and to facilitate effective behavior in the learning community, we recommend working with students to create class agreements that emphasize and prioritize a supportive environment. As Taylor described doing with her students in this chapter's instructional snapshot, this practice can play an integral role in building a supportive learning community and in clearly establishing expectations that can be used to help guide effective behavior throughout the remainder of the school year. When you talk with your students about the ideas and expectations that go into these agreements, we encourage you to focus on ideas related to inclusivity, acceptance, and equity (as Taylor did with her students). By prioritizing the importance of these concepts to the class community's agreements, we educators can work with our students to create learning environments that help students feel comfortable, included, and valued.

One way to guide these discussions and maximize their effectiveness is to align them with books that the class reads together. For example, this chapter's instructional snapshot refers to Taylor reading *The Day You Begin* by Jaqueline Woodson, *Those Shoes* by Maribeth Boelts, and *Just Ask* by Sonia Sotomayor; by reading these works to her students, Taylor helped the students reflect on important topics that could inform their ideas about community expectations. In the context of remote learning, it's especially important for us as educators to be thoughtful and purposeful about the topics addressed in our class agreements: we want to focus on concepts that are relevant to ways students will interact with each other in this educational setting. We believe that class expectations that prioritize a supportive environment will help students feel comfortable in the remote learning environment and display positive behaviors when interacting with their classmates and teachers.

Adapting for a Range of Modalities

We know that remote and distance learning takes a wide range of forms and is conducted using a variety of modalities. In this section, we describe key ideas to consider when implementing the chapter's key insights in different forms of remote instruction, focusing specifically on entirely remote instruction (in which instruction is completely virtual), hybrid instruction (in which students are physically present in the classroom some days and engage through virtual learning other days), and hyflex instruction (in which some students are physically present in the classroom and other students join at the same time virtually). While many of the community-building recommendations described in this chapter are applicable regardless of the learning modality, we share some important points to keep in mind related to each instructional form.

Instructional Modality	Key Suggestions to Consider
Entirely remote	Use the features of remote learning to work for you as you build a community: utilize online tools such as the Zoom chat box, Google Docs, and Google Slides to communicate with your students, share information that is relevant to you, and create opportunities to do the same.
Hybrid	Remember that in hybrid instruction, you will be constructing two communities: the online community and the face-to-face version. Some of the features of the face-to-face community may not convey to the online version and vice versa. Because of this, we recommend using both in-person and online community-building strategies. For example, you can use the features of remote learning described in the previous suggestion to construct an online-learning community while using face-to-face interactions and conversations to create a cohesive face-to-face learning environment.
Hyflex	Since the hyflex format involves engaging with students through online and in-person instruction at the same time, it's important to construct a learning community that provides equal opportunities for participation and engagement with both audiences. For example, when checking in with students or modeling your ideas, be sure

Instructional Modality	Key Suggestions to Consider
	that you're communicating in ways to which both groups can feel connected. This can sometimes be as simple as making sure you make eye contact with the students in the class and with the camera that corresponds with what virtual students see. You can also share information through formats that all students can access whether they are in the classroom or in another setting; Google Docs and Google Slides can facilitate these interactions.

2

Class Discussion and Student Collaboration in a New Era

The ideas in this chapter extend from the insights presented in Chapter One. While that chapter described the process of constructing a learning community in remote instruction, this chapter discusses important classroom activities that are facilitated by a strong learning community: class discussion and student collaboration. These instructional tactics, which we consider essential to effective language arts instruction, can be challenging to implement in remote learning but are especially significant to maximizing students' learning experiences (Hurst, Wallace, & Nixon, 2013; Kyei-Blankson, Ntuli, & Donnelly, 2019). We first explore what it means to facilitate class discussion and student collaboration in the new era of remote instruction, noting specific attributes, challenges, and opportunities associated with these activities. Next, we reflect on why class discussion and student collaboration in remote learning are so important, which we follow with an instructional snapshot section that provides an example of Taylor's work with her elementary school students. Then we share key recommendations for teachers to consider when facilitating class discussions and student collaboration in remote language arts instruction. Finally, we discuss how the ideas described in this chapter can be utilized in and adapted for a wide range of modalities.

What Does It Mean to Facilitate Class Discussion and Student Collaboration in Remote Instruction?

Remote learning has caused us language arts teachers to rethink the concepts of discussion and collaboration. When we (Sean and Taylor) constructed our pre-pandemic in-person learning environments, we did so with the idea that students would be able to see one other in person during discussions and that they'd be able to be positioned relatively closely (such as at the same table or desk cluster) during collaborative work. Once we moved to remote instruction, we knew we needed to make important decisions about discussion and collaboration that were informed by the features of remote learning and by our beliefs about effective teaching. Based on our beliefs that discussion and collaboration are essential aspects of language arts instruction, we looked for methods and practices to ensure that our students could still discuss their insights and work together on relevant activities in remote contexts.

While we knew that some aspects of remote discussion and collaboration would be different, we wanted to ensure that our learning environments maintained certain key attributes of these components:

◆ We wanted students to be able to express their ideas with classmates in ways that foster an inclusive and open classroom environment.
◆ We wanted students to be able to learn from one another and to continue to develop their abilities to thoughtfully respond to others' perspectives.
◆ We wanted students to benefit academically, socially, and personally from collaborative work by participating in communal processes of meaning-making, communicating, and benefiting from their classmates' insights.

In order to put these principles into action in remote learning, we reflected on concepts such as our students' access to technological resources, the instructional modalities our schools were using, and the tools that we felt would best allow us to facilitate meaningful collaboration and discussion. Using collaborative tools such as Google Docs and Slides, Zoom features such as chat functions and breakout groups, and asynchronous online discussions, we created a variety of opportunities for our students to engage in inclusive, supportive, and academically meaningful collaboration.

We knew that constructing opportunities for our students to discuss course material and work collaboratively would be a challenge, but we felt it was an essential aspect of language arts learning. These resources and tools provided us with a number of opportunities to create student-centered discussion opportunities for our students as they interacted with and learned from one another. In the next section, we reflect further on why class discussion and student collaboration are so important to effective remote teaching and learning of language arts.

Why Is This Important?

Class discussion and student collaboration are important to strong remote language arts instruction for a number of research-based reasons that are immediately applicable to teaching in today's context. First, it's important to note that discussion and collaboration have been shown to increase students' learning in language arts in a range of ways, as these experiences promote problem-solving abilities, enhance comprehension, develop social skills, and help students develop other important abilities (Hurst et al., 2013). The effect of these activities on students' learning experiences illustrates that we educators can maximize the benefits of the work we do with our students when we create opportunities for them to work together and share ideas.

Another point of particular significance to this chapter and to today's educational context is that collaboration, interaction, and discussion are especially important to the quality of students' experiences in remote instruction (Kyei-Blankson et al., 2019). Kyei-Blankson and colleagues (2019) discuss the importance of encouraging and cultivating students' "social presence" in online learning, explaining that "social presence occurs when the learners are able to project themselves in the course as real people interacting with other members" (p. 53). By creating opportunities for students in our language arts classes to work collaboratively, share insights, and discuss their insights, we can help maximize their social presence, which will maximize their abilities to learn and the effectiveness of their experiences.

It's also important to point out that remote collaboration and discussion has features and benefits that are not present in the traditional face-to-face version of these practices; for example, asynchronous communication and discussion (such as the kinds facilitated by online discussion boards) give students the opportunity to work through ideas at their own pace and center students, instead of the teacher, in the communication that takes place (Grisham & Wolsey, 2006). In addition, other forms of remote discussion and interaction can have similar benefits by circumventing the typical classroom communication dynamic: when students share ideas remotely through Zoom features, such as chat boxes and breakout rooms, and Google programs, such as Google Docs and Slides, they do not need to have the same level of comfort with in-person communication. Students may or may not be comfortable with sharing ideas verbally in the traditional classrooms setting for a variety of reasons, such as the size of the class, their confidence in the material, the amount of time available, and their previous experiences in school, and variety of personal attributes; the technology-based interaction and collaboration made necessary by remote instruction can provide all students with varied, decentralized, democratic, and differentiated opportunities to discuss ideas and collaborate with their peers (Rhine & Bailey, 2011).

To maximize our students' learning experiences (in language arts in general and in remote instruction in particular), it's essential that we create opportunities for our students to collaborate with one another and discuss their insights. In the next section, we take a look at an example of Taylor's work facilitating interaction and collaboration in her elementary school language arts classes.

Instructional Snapshot: An Example From Taylor's Work

The Google Suite is a holy grail for collaboration. Even as we write this work, we are collaborating over Google Docs. Many schools use Google Chromebooks, allowing access to Google Suite tools. My school district is lucky enough to have 1:1 Chromebooks for each student starting in kindergarten. The district also enforces technology usage heavily, so even before we were forced into the emergency virtual learning caused by COVID-19, we were using technology and digital collaboration.

For teachers who do not have this same luxury but want to use the same collaboration methods, it is critical to model what behaviors you expect throughout the experience. Teachers will have to prepare for collaboration experiences but the value goes far beyond any annoyance that may occur.

Early in our summarizing lessons, the students discussed "summary statements" and how to create them based on a short paragraph they were given. We did one example together and worked through the Who, When/Where, and What Happened. I modeled what that looked like and then divided the students into breakout rooms. Breakout rooms are a wonderful tool from Zoom that allows us to break up students into smaller groups into smaller Zoom sessions, but I can still jump in and out of each room. Thankfully, my class is full of diverse learners, anywhere from gifted and talented students to students with individualized education plans (IEPs), and this allows us to have successful heterogeneous groups when we split into those breakout rooms.

Thanks to Google Slides, the students were all able to collaborate on a one-slide document. This was nice because all the students were working on one document; therefore, they were all seeing changes in real time. This also allowed me to monitor all four groups as they made their summary statements even if I wasn't in their specific breakout room at the time. When the groups were done, they came back to the "whole group" Zoom session, and we discussed the summary statements of each group.

Breakout rooms and Google Slides allow teachers and students to have meaningful experiences when collaborating virtually. It's no lie that collaboration in the virtual classroom looks different from the traditional classroom, but with these tools, group work can continue. It was very critical that when learning in that virtual environment, I figured out a way to ensure collaboration among my students.

Key Recommendations

In this section, we share and discuss key recommendations to consider when facilitating class discussions and student collaboration in your own remote language arts instruction. These suggestions are designed to help you as you put the ideas and insights described in this chapter into practice:

◆ Strategically utilize a wide range of collaboration and discussion methods.
◆ Explain both the how and the why of discussion and collaboration tools.
◆ Emphasize respect during student discussions and collaborations.
◆ Provide students with choice and ownership regarding their collaborations and discussions.

Incorporating these recommendations will help you construct interactive, thoughtful, and student-centered discussions and collaborations that will help students achieve the maximum benefit from these important activities. In addition, they will guide you as you consider how to convey your ideas and beliefs about effective language arts discussions and collaborations to the remote context. Now, let's take a look at each of these suggestions in more detail.

Recommendation One: Strategically Utilize a Wide Range of Collaboration and Discussion Methods

There are two important components of this recommendation: the first is to incorporate a variety of methods when creating opportunities for students to have discussions and work collaboratively, and the second is to select those collaboration and discussion methods strategically based on how well they align with the purpose of that task. By putting these ideas into action, we ensure that we are providing our students with a wide range of ways to engage with each other and that those interaction forms are aligned with the kinds of collaboration and discussion in which they're engaging. When we're planning ways for our students to interact, we want to keep them active and engaged with a variety of methods and activities: depending in part on the modalities we're using, we might ask students to share responses verbally through Zoom, write a comment in a chat box, or work collaboratively on Google Docs and/or Google Slides.

However, this variety is associated with more than just keeping students interested: we also want to consider a range of collaboration and discussion options so that we can select the method that best aligns with our instructional goal. For example, we might ask students in a Zoom meeting to share a short response through the chat box, while a longer response or collaborative activity would be better suited for a Google Doc. In addition, if we want students to be able to think about classmates' responses outside of the scheduled class meeting, we can create asynchronous discussion boards that align with this purpose. By closely aligning our instructional goals with the discussion and collaboration methods we ask our students to use, we can ensure that the connection between the form and function of the tools we're using.

Recommendation Two: Explain Both the How and the Why of Discussion and Collaboration Tools

Since the collaboration and discussion tools used in remote language arts instruction can be unfamiliar to some students and different from what they may have previously used for these purposes, we recommend talking early in the school year with students about how to implement the discussion and collaboration tools you're utilizing. This can be done during the same time you go over other procedures and guidelines that are essential to student success; for example, you might introduce some of the resources and programs you'll use to facilitate collaboration and discussion, model their use for students, and provide them with some especially important tips to keep in mind when using it on their own. By doing this, we can help students feel comfortable using the resources—which can, in turn, help students feel more likely to engage during discussions and collaborations.

In addition to showing students how to implement tools and resources used for discussion and collaboration, we recommend talking with students about *why* they'll be using those tools. By sharing (in age and developmentally aligned ways) with students the reasons they'll be using certain resources for particular types of discussion and collaboration, we can create an atmosphere of transparency and clear communication in our instruction.

For example, before we ask students to use online discussion boards, we can share with them the benefits of using these boards and types of discussion for which they'll use them. We can then compare that resource with another type, such as Google Slides, highlighting the kinds of collaboration for which that tool will be used. These kinds of discussions provide students with the clarity that comes from purposeful technology use (Young & Bush, 2004) and can help them feel comfortable engaging with these tools and resources during remote learning.

Remember that students will get excited if you get excited. One of the things students are missing when experiencing learning totally remotely is social interaction; by sharing with them the possibilities of breakout rooms, Google Suite collaboration tools, and the like, they are able to engage in professional, but social, interactions that make learning more meaningful and fun.

Recommendation Three: Emphasize Respect During Student Discussions and Collaborations

To maximize the effectiveness of students' experiences collaborating and discussing information in the remote language arts setting, we strongly recommend emphasizing respectful and supportive communication during these collaborative activities. There are certainly legitimate concerns about young people communicating in harmful ways online, which has led to an increased focus on teaching youth about digital citizenship, which includes respectful and supportive online communication (Jones & Mitchell, 2016). Since much of remote learning, discussion, and collaboration involve the use of digital communication tools, we believe it is important for teachers to talk with students about key attributes of effective digital citizenship.

Teachers can model effective digital communication for students by showing them what respectful collaboration can look like. For instance, a teacher might respond to a student's discussion board post with an example of what a supportive and respectful reply looks like. The teacher could then think aloud for students about the comment's specific supportive and respectful aspects and then use that information to launch a conversation with students about what they can do to ensure they can respond to others in positive ways. Teachers and students could work together to create a set of expectations for respectful collaboration that can be posted on the class's learning management system (such as Blackboard, Canvas, or Google Classroom). The teacher can then periodically remind students of these expectations to help ensure respectful collaboration and discussion.

A lot of times, our K–6 students simply do not understand professionalism because it is not something they have had to practice before. It is imperative that you allow space for students to make mistakes and encourage them to learn from them. Taylor always does a fun "game" in order to teach appropriate social interactions and accountable talk in the first week of school, and this can be easily adapted for collaborations. For example, the teacher could post something on a discussion board and have the students purposely write something they KNOW isn't professional or kind (obviously, something that is still appropriate for school). This allows the teacher to work with the students to turn it into something positive and have a lesson about accountable talk. Students get a laugh out of poking fun at their teacher with permission, and the teacher slides in a lesson without the kids even knowing it!

Recommendation Four: Provide Students With Choice and Ownership Regarding Their Collaborations and Discussions

In order to maximize the quality of and engagement associated with students' collaborative work and discussions, we recommend providing opportunities for choice and ownership. The choice and ownership the teacher provides will vary based on the specific work students are doing at a particular time and can take a variety of forms, such as opportunities to choose the format through which they collaborate, the content they discuss, or a combination of the two. When providing students with choice, we believe it's important to provide a combination of teacher guidance and student freedom. In other words, we want to provide students with clear expectations for an assignment while still giving them as much opportunity as possible to individualize their work.

For example, if students are working collaboratively in a jigsaw activity in which each group shares what they noticed about a key section or story element, groups could have the opportunity to select how they collaborate and share the results of their works: they could work together and display their ideas through Google Docs, Google Slides, or another collaborative tool. They could also make choices related to the content they discuss, such as which aspects of a particular section most stood out to them and why. Similarly, we can provide students with choice and ownership in the ideas they share in whole-class discussions about texts they've read by asking them to make personal connections between their own lives, issues that matter to them, and other works they've read and the content in the pieces. In addition, since students may be more comfortable sharing these ideas through different tools and mediums, we can take this form of individualization into account by allowing students to share their ideas verbally, through a Zoom chat function or through another tool. These opportunities for individualization can help students feel a sense of ownership over their collaboration and discussion experiences.

In Taylor's class, she has a few IEP/504 accommodations whereby these choices are necessary when planning each lesson. Much like the Universal Design for Learning suggests, things can be done for kids with special needs that can help out all students. When Taylor has the students discuss or share, she often has them do it through FlipGrid. FlipGrid is an awesome tool that lets students record short videos in response to a question. Some students do not love the idea of recording themselves, so she gives them a discussion board option as well and allows each child to choose what is best for them. Usually, Taylor has about half her class choose both options, allowing her to get the best assessment of what they really know because they're comfortable in the choice they made.

Adapting for a Range of Modalities

When reflecting on class discussions and opportunities for student collaboration in remote learning, it's important to consider the range of modalities through which remote language arts instruction is conducted. In this section, we share ideas to consider when implementing the chapter's insights in different forms of remote instruction, focusing specifically on entirely remote instruction (in which instruction is completely virtual), hybrid instruction (in which students are physically present in the classroom some days and engage through virtual learning other days), and hyflex instruction (in which some students are physically present in the classroom and other students join at the same time virtually). It's important to note that the core attributes of collaboration and discussion and the key associated recommendations described in this chapter can be applied no matter the modality. The modality adaptations discussed in this section are designed to help you think through the features of the instructional format you use and how it aligns with the principles of effective collaboration and discussion.

Instructional Modality	Key Suggestions to Consider
Entirely remote	If you are teaching entirely remotely, we encourage you to reflect on all the collaboration and discussion tools available to you and your students. You might even make a list of the online tools you can have access to and are comfortable with, noting the features of those tools and the kinds of collaboration and discussion they can facilitate. In addition, since your students will be engaging with each other entirely online, we recommend spending time discussing the features of digital citizenship to ensure that students will communicate respectfully.
Hybrid	Since students in hybrid instruction will take part in virtual learning some days and in-person interaction on other days, it's important to keep both of these types of interaction in mind while planning collaboration and discussion, since some discussion and collaboration methods will be more aligned with in-person discussions and others with remote idea exchanges. Because of this, we recommend being particularly strategic and mindful of the way the class is meeting when making decisions about discussion and collaboration.
Hyflex	Because hyflex instruction calls for some students to join the class online at the same time that others are present in person, it's important to keep both groups of students in mind when constructing opportunities for collaboration and discussion. There are multiple ways that we educators can do this; one tactic is to create opportunities for all students in the course (whether they join a particular meeting through an online platform like Zoom or if they're present in person) to use technological collaboration tools like Google Docs and Google Slides to interact. This can allow all students in the class to work collaboratively and maximize the opportunities for discussion among the students.

II

The Potential of Remote Language Arts Instruction

3

A New Format of Writing and Grammar Instruction

In this chapter, we look closely at the best ways to teach writing and grammar in the context of remote language arts instruction. While teaching writing and grammar remotely can certainly be challenging, we also feel that the remote environment provides a number of opportunities for innovative and engaging instruction in this aspect of language arts. Through the information in this chapter, we convey essential aspects of effective writing and grammar instruction and provide suggestions to consider when working with your students remotely on these instructional components. We begin by first exploring key components of remote writing and grammar instruction, identifying its major attributes and the challenges and opportunities associated with it. Next, we reflect on why it's so important to effectively teach grammar and writing in remote contexts, which we follow with an instructional snapshot section that provides an example of Taylor's work with her elementary school students. Then, we share key recommendations for teachers to consider when teaching writing and grammar remotely. Finally, we discuss how the ideas in this chapter can be implemented in a range of modalities.

What Are the Key Aspects of Remote Writing and Grammar Instruction?

When we reflect on effective writing and grammar instruction, we think of an active process for students and teachers. We picture strategy-focused mini-lessons, discussions of mentor texts, engaged students working on drafts, conferences between students and teachers, and other demonstrations of active learning. While the specific methods of delivery and collaboration will certainly differ, we feel that all these components of effective writing instruction can be achieved in remote learning. Through the purposeful and strategic use of technological resources, we educators can provide students with writing instruction that represents its research-based best practices. We believe remote teaching and learning can align with key components of student-centered writing instruction: remote instruction that utilizes short, focused periods of direct instruction on a platform such as Google Meet or Zoom, followed by opportunities for students to work on their own pieces of writing allows students to engage in writing instruction in active ways.

For example, in their book *Writing Workshop: The Essential Guide*, Fletcher and Portalupi (2001) compare strong writing instruction to an industrial arts class or to ski lessons in which the instructor models and explains a concept or strategy and then creates opportunities for the students to try it out on their own, checking in with them individually while doing so. Remote writing and grammar instruction, we believe, can provide this same student-focused context in which our students work on their writing and teachers check in with and support them as they do so. The modalities might be different than what many of us are used to, but we can still apply the principles of strong writing instruction to remote learning. When teaching grammatical concepts in the context of writing instruction, for instance, we educators can apply the same best practices of focused mini-lessons and mentor text use that we would apply in the face-to-face classroom. In this chapter, we further explore the significance of these instructional practices and ways to put them into action in the language arts classroom.

Why Is It Important?

While there are certainly challenges associated with it, we strongly believe in the importance of remote instruction that aligns with the best practices of teaching writing and grammar. By creating opportunities for our students to examine mentor texts, apply writing strategies in authentic ways, receive individualized instruction from us, and share work with real-world audiences, we can provide students with outstanding writing instruction, which is essential to students' success in many aspects of their lives (National Writing Project & Nagin, 2006). In the book *Because Writing Matters*, the National Writing Project and Carl Nagin (2006) assert that effective writing instruction is so important to our students for a range of reasons: "in today's increasingly diverse society, writing is a gateway for success in academia, the new workplace, and the global economy, as well as for our collective success as a participatory democracy" (p. 2).

Additional resources published since *Because Writing Matters* continue to comment and elaborate on the importance of effective writing skills in today's society; for example, the 2016 National Council of Teachers of English (NCTE) document *Professional Knowledge for the Teaching of Writing* explains that our students' writing skills are essential to their successes in a number of important contexts. Among the ideas in this NCTE piece that highlight the significance of writing to our students' lives are assertions that writing in today's society takes a number of forms: writing is done for audiences and purposes beyond school, students' abilities to write are important to their abilities to participate in society, writing can be used to enhance students' personal growth, and digital environments have created new audiences and opportunities for writing. Now, in today's world, we can put the research-based insights in *Because Writing Matters* and NCTE's *Professional Knowledge for the Teaching of Writing* into action by connecting them with the features and attributes of remote learning. By providing our students with strong remote writing instruction that applies the best practices of teaching writing to distance learning, we can help them develop essential skills for their personal, academic, and career success.

Now, let's take a look at an example of Taylor's work with the students in her class as she engages them in remote writing instruction.

Instructional Snapshot: An Example From Taylor's Work

Every year we are asked to complete a performance task straight from our school's preferred writing program. Of the 13 teachers I have directly worked with in the last two years, not a single one of them actually liked the performance tasks, making it difficult to make the instruction meaningful for our students. When we were slapped in the face with the pandemic and the virtual instruction that came with it, we expected that the school district would take away its expectations for the performance task—*we were wrong*. And thus, we had to make the instruction not only meaningful for our students but something we could do virtually as well.

The performance task consists of five parts: notes on one source, notes on another source, research questions, rough draft, and final draft. Usually, we model the first performance task of the year, we do the second one together, and then the last one they do individually—the classic "I do, we do, you do" method. In order to do this, we had to digitize everything, which took some time, but since we were able to stick them right into Schoology, the students were able to easily access everything. We uploaded each part of the performance task to a Google Slides presentation—which we shared with each of the students—and put "stop sign" clip art between each day's work.

We got through the notes process and the research questions in four days, rather than the three days we had originally allotted. *First rule of remote learning: don't stress about pacing. Ultimately, your students will get what they need.* After that, it was time for them to begin their rough draft. In order to thoroughly prepare the students for their rough draft, we discussed what each paragraph should look like as I recorded on a Google Doc while sharing my screen. This allowed the students to have accountability over their rough drafts, rather than just giving them an outline. Most students finished their rough drafts within the day since they had an hour of uninterrupted writing time, and the notes and research questions acted as a brainstorm. Because of this, I was able to dip into their own Google Docs and add comments to their rough drafts. This allowed me to "confer" with each of my students without having to spend valuable teaching time with each student. Instead, I was able to add comments to all their writing and then instruct the students to either move on to their final draft, revise/edit and resubmit, or set up a time for a writing conference in Zoom breakout rooms with me. My students are pretty good writers, so most did not have to meet with me "personally," but those who did found value in the meeting.

My students ended up producing amazing final drafts. The prompt was asking them to describe a trip to Washington, D.C., by choosing three memorials to talk about and describe. I always tell my students to be as creative as possible when it comes to these because the monotonous and repetitive writings get quite hard to grade, especially with 22 student papers to flip through. One student wrote the whole paper like a news report. Another one wrote about how the Demogorgon attacked when he got to the Martin Luther King, Jr. Memorial. After dreading the performance task, I ended up having a blast reading and grading their final drafts, and a lot of the students had a good time writing their stories as well.

Key Recommendations

In this section, we provide and describe key recommendations to keep in mind regarding remote writing and grammar instruction. Following these suggestions will help you put the best practices of teaching writing and grammar into action in remote contexts, providing your students with the instruction, insights, and support that will help them write effectively:

◆ Conduct short, focused mini-lessons on the features of specific writing strategies and grammatical concepts.

◆ Use mentor texts to illustrate how published authors use these strategies and concepts authentically.

◆ Help students analyze the importance of writing strategies and grammatical concepts to effective writing.

◆ Use technological collaboration tools to confer with students as they apply writing strategies and grammatical concepts to their own works.

◆ Ask students to reflect on how specific strategies and concepts enhance the effectiveness of their writings.

By utilizing these ideas, you'll provide your students with strategic writing instruction that presents key strategies and concepts as tools for effective writing, purposefully utilizes mentor texts, creates opportunities for students to apply writing strategies and concepts to their own works, and helps students reflect on the impact these writing tools have on their own works. Now, we describe these recommendations in more detail, discussing their applications to remote teaching and learning.

Recommendation One: Conduct Short, Focused Mini-Lessons on the Features of Specific Writing Strategies and Grammatical Concepts

We recommend beginning the process of effective remote grammar and writing instruction with short, focused mini-lessons on specific strategies and concepts. Whether we deliver these mini-lessons synchronously through live instruction on a platform like Google Meet or Zoom or asynchronously through a recorded video that we create and make available for our students (or a combination of both, such as a live lesson on Zoom that we record for students to have access to later), we can use these brief and informative explanations to introduce students to important components of effective writing and describe for them the key features of those strategies. Regardless of the specific modality used to remotely present these mini-lessons, we suggest using the mini-lessons to describe to students what a particular writing strategy or grammatical concept is and why it is important to effective writing. This instructional approach will help students see these strategies and concepts as tools of strong writing, thereby preparing them for the subsequent steps of the instructional process in which students ultimately apply the strategies they learn to their own works and reflect on those strategies' impacts.

As you prepare the mini-lessons you'll present to your students, we recommend structuring the content of each lesson in three sections: (1) What is the writing strategy or grammatical concept being discussed? (2) What are its key features? and (3) Why is it important to effective writing? The first question is not only the most fundamental, as it focuses on what the mini-lesson is describing, but also very important: by clearly identifying the topic of a mini-lesson while planning it, we can ensure that we're giving students clear and focused instruction that addresses a specific aspect of writing. For example, a strong mini-lesson on sensory detail would clearly identify its focal topic and convey that topic to students early in the lesson. The second question calls for us as teachers to explain to students the essential aspects of the lesson's topic to students. Continuing with the example of sensory detail, a lesson on this topic would describe for students in clear and concise ways what sensory detail is, providing information on the ways authors use language to appeal to readers' senses. Finally, the third question helps build students' understanding of the significance of the focal concept by sharing reasons authors might use the topic to maximize the effectiveness of their works. When describing sensory language, for example, we can share with students some reasons why authors choose to use that concept, focusing on ideas such as the ways it allows readers to deeply understand a particular scene or event in ways that stand out to them.

Recommendation Two: Use Mentor Texts to Illustrate How Published Authors Use These Strategies and Concepts Authentically

Once you've shared with students a brief mini-lesson that focuses on the key aspects of a particular writing strategy or grammatical concept, we recommend building on that information by sharing with students one or more published mentor texts in which the focal strategy is effectively used. Sharing published examples of key writing strategies and grammatical concepts provides students with a number of important benefits: (1) it provides them with concrete examples of what specific writing strategies and grammatical concepts look like in authentic situations; (2) it can increase students' "buy-in" to the concept or strategy by showing them that it is used in real-world contexts, not just in classroom activities or on worksheets; and (3) it can further engage students in the material, especially when they examine examples from texts that are of high interest to them.

When selecting examples to share with your students, we encourage you to ask yourself three questions: (1) Is it a clear example of the focal writing strategy or grammatical concept? (2) Is the example from a text aligned with the students' general reading level? and (3) Is the example from a text that students in the class may find interesting, relevant, or engaging? If you can answer yes to these three questions, then that text would be a great mentor text to use with your students! For example, you might select the following example from R.J. Palacio's (2012) novel *Wonder*—in which the book's protagonist, Auggie, describes an administrator's office in his new school—as an example of sensory detail if you feel the text is aligned with your students' general reading level and potentially engaging to them:

> I was looking around at all the things on his desk. Cool stuff, like a globe that floated in the air and a Rubik's-type cube made with little mirrors. I like his office a lot. I liked that there were all these neat little drawings and paintings by students on the walls, framed like they were important.
>
> (p. 19)

The sensory details in this passage provide a clear model of what this writing strategy looks like in the context of a published text, which can help convey to students the role the strategy plays in authentic writing done by published authors.

Oftentimes, students will pull things from stories they have read and will point them out to you! Taylor often has students come up to her and share they are writing something (whether for fun or to fulfill an assignment) where they came up with whatever motif they picked up from the author. Because of this, Taylor always left out the books they had recently read for students to get their hands on in the classroom. Virtually, I stick YouTube videos of the books in a folder on Schoology so that the students can go back and watch the book again if they want to look back at the books we have read.

There are a variety of ways to use the features of remote learning to share mentor texts with students. As with the mini-lessons described in the previous recommendation, we teachers can share these texts synchronously through a format such as Zoom or Google Meet, asynchronously through a recorded video, or through a combination (such as a live lesson that is recorded and made available for reference later on). When sharing mentor texts remotely, we recommend placing the text of the selected passage on your screen by either transcribing it or sharing an image of the text and sharing the screen with your students. As you share these examples, we advise reading the passage aloud as your students follow along. While doing so, we suggest thinking aloud for your students about how the author uses the focal concept or strategy, modeling your thought process about what you notice regarding the author's use of the strategy, the impact it has on the effectiveness of the piece, and why you think the author chose to use that concept. Doing this will give students an example of how to look at and reflect on a mentor text that effectively uses a specific writing strategy. This knowledge will prepare students for the third component of this instructional process, described in the next recommendation.

Recommendation Three: Help Students Analyze the Importance of Writing Strategies and Grammatical Concepts to Effective Writing

At this stage of the instructional process, students work to analyze the importance of the focal strategy to effective writing. While you'll still provide students with support and guidance, this step gives increased ownership and responsibility to students: it represents a shift from the teacher discussing the features and impact of a particular writing strategy or grammatical concept to the students analyzing its significance. While there are a variety of ways to organize the specifics of this activity based on particular instructional modalities and other aspects, the core components are that students look at a published text, analyze the author's use of the focal strategy, and reflect on how and why the author chose to use that strategy.

Because of the many ways students can engage in this activity, it aligns well with remote learning. For example, you might share with your students an electronic file of a short story and ask each student to select an example of the strategy or concept on which you're focusing that day. This activity can also be easily done in groups: students could use Zoom breakout rooms or a similar resource to work together to find examples and analyze the importance of the focal strategy. When facilitating group work on this activity, you could provide each group with a separate text or have all the groups use the same text for the activity.

We recommend implementing this activity in a variety of ways to keep students engaged and to demonstrate all of the different ways that this type of analysis can take place. In addition, creating a range of opportunities for students to analyze writing strategies and grammatical concepts will allow them to purposefully use the tools of remote learning in a number of context-specific ways, giving them a range of opportunities to engage with content and with varying technological resources. Whether students work independently or in groups, we suggest asking them to share their findings at the conclusion of the activity. This celebrates students' work, allows students to learn from each other, and creates opportunities for you as the teacher to address any misunderstandings or confusion.

Text You Used	Example of the Focal Strategy or Concept in the Text	Why You Feel the Strategy or Concept Is Important to the Effectiveness of the Text

Figure 3.1 Graphic Organizer for Published Text Analysis

The graphic organizer depicted in Figure 3.1 (also available in Appendix A) provides a useful resource for students as they analyze the importance of a writing strategy or grammatical concept to the effectiveness of a published text. We recommend making electronic copies of the resource available for students so they can use it to record their identifications and insights while working on this activity.

Recommendation Four: Use Technological Collaboration Tools to Confer With Students as They Apply Writing Strategies and Grammatical Concepts to Their Own Works

Now that students have learned about the features of key writing strategies and grammatical concepts, examined mentor texts, and analyzed the importance of focal strategies and concepts to published examples, it's time to provide them with an opportunity to put the ideas they've learned into practice in their own writing. To do this, we recommend creating instructional time dedicated to students working on their own writing projects. Building this independent writing time into your instruction gives them time to use the writing strategies and grammatical concepts they've been learning about it in class. In addition, it varies the instructional modality moving away from a typical Zoom- or Google Meet–style lesson and to a writing workshop structure that focuses on students' individual works as writers. Depending on your curriculum, the projects students create during this time can be works of students' choice, assigned topics, or a combination of the two.

Regardless of the specific pieces they are writing, we suggest holding individual conferences with students to monitor their progress and provide individualized instruction (Myroup, 2020). In these conferences, we recommend talking with each student about the piece they're writing, asking them questions about their goals for the work, noting its specific strengths, and identifying a specific way for the writer to continue to develop it. We suggest incorporating the focal strategy or concept that the class has been discussing into the conference conversation but not limiting the discussion to that topic. Instead, we encourage you to look at all aspects of each student's work so that you can provide each of them with specific and individualized insights about their writing.

One-on-one writing conferences can still be effectively utilized in remote learning, although they will take somewhat different forms than they would in an in-person, non–socially distanced classroom. Instead of sitting down at a table with a student to hold a conference, we can use technological collaboration tools to adapt our conferences for remote learning. One effective tactic for holding remote writing conferences with students is to place each student in their own Zoom breakout room during their independent writing time. Then, to confer with a student, you'll join their individual breakout room and hold a one-on-one conference with them about the piece they're writing. We like this method of conferring because of the opportunities it provides for conversation and clarification. If you're unable to communicate with students through a platform like Zoom because of technological issues, another way to hold a remote conference is by using Google Docs to have a text-based conversation in which you ask them questions about their work, identify specific strengths, and note particular suggestions for improvement. If you use this text-based model, we encourage you to be sure to communicate with students about their work by asking them questions and waiting for responses before giving them suggestions for improvement; this exchange of ideas can help you understand students' goals and interests, which can allow you to individualize your feedback to that individual student.

Regardless of the specific technological tools used in a one-on-one writing conference, we recommend using a graphic organizer to record the information discussed in the conference and keep track of student progress. You can

Student's name:

Date:

The day's focal strategy:

Title and Brief Description of the Student's Piece	A Specific Strength of the Piece You Identified	A Concrete Suggestion for Improvement You Shared With the Student

Figure 3.2 Writing Conference Graphic Organizer

keep an electronic file for each student containing the graphic organizer from each conference you had with them, which will provide a great deal of formative assessment data and documentation of their writing development. One example of a graphic organizer you could use for this purpose is depicted in Figure 3.2; this organizer asks for the student's name, the date, the day's focal strategy, the title and a brief description of the piece the student is writing, a strength of the piece you identified, and a concrete suggestion for improvement you shared with the student.

Recommendation Five: Ask Students to Reflect On How Specific Strategies and Concepts Enhance the Effectiveness of Their Writings

We recommend concluding these steps by asking students to reflect on the focal strategy on which you and the students have been focusing throughout the instructional process. To facilitate students' reflections, we suggest asking them two related questions, each one designed to promote thoughtful analysis of the importance of specific grammatical concepts and writing strategies to effective writing. First, we recommend asking students how the focal strategy enhanced the writing they did that day. For example, if the class was focused on the use of sensory detail, you could ask the students, "How did the sensory details you used in your piece enhance the effectiveness of your work?" In addition, we suggest asking students to reflect on how they think their work would be different if they didn't use the focal strategy. When studying sensory detail, you might ask, "How do you think your piece would be different if you didn't use sensory detail in it?" By responding to these questions, students will think carefully and analytically about the impact of the focal writing strategy or grammatical concept, which can help them further understand how that strategy or concept can function as a tool that writers use to enhance the quality of their works.

There are a variety of ways students can share these reflections while utilizing the features of remote learning. One especially effective practice is to ask students to use a shared Google Doc to share their responses. After students reflect individually on the questions, they can look at their peers' answers and note similarities and differences between their insights on the importance of the focal strategy and their classmates' ideas. Once they've done that, students can interact further with their peers by writing positive comments under their classmates' responses, such as similarities in the responses or new ideas they gained from someone else's insights. If you would prefer students respond to you individually, you can ask them to submit these ideas directly to you through an assignment in your learning management system, such as Canvas, Blackboard, Google Classroom, or another similar system. No matter how you organize students' submissions, these reflection questions will help students reflect on the importance of key writing strategies and grammatical concepts while also providing a meaningful sense of closure to this instructional process.

Adapting for a Range of Modalities

Since remote language arts instruction is conducted by different individuals using a range of modalities, this section shares ideas to consider when implementing this chapter's insights on effective writing and grammar instruction in varying forms of remote instruction. In it, we describe insights to consider when implementing the chapter's points about effective writing and grammar instruction in a range of modes: entirely remote instruction (in which instruction is completely virtual), hybrid instruction (in which students are physically present in the classroom some days and engage through virtual learning other days), and hyflex instruction (in which some students are physically present in the classroom and other students join at the same time virtually). The modality adaptations discussed here are designed to provide you with additional support and recommendations as you help your students understand that writing strategies and grammar concepts are tools that authors use purposefully to maximize the impacts of their works.

Instructional Modality	Key Suggestions to Consider
Entirely remote	Entirely remote writing instruction aligns with a variety of ways for students to use technological tools and resources to learn, collaborate, and share. We encourage you to think about the online tools to which you have access, with which you are comfortable, and that will facilitate the instructional components of this process. For instance, we suggest identifying the best ways for you to deliver remote mini-lessons and mentor text explanations, the collaboration tools that you think will most effectively allow your students to work together on text analyses, and the technological resources that will best facilitate individual writing conferences. As you select these technological tools, we encourage you to keep in mind that some students may have varying levels of internet access, so there may be situations in which you might need to choose alternative options that do not require high-speed internet.
Hybrid	Because students engaging in hybrid instruction participate in virtual learning on some days and in-person classes on others, the most important aspect of planning for this modality is to reflect on which strategies and tools align best with in-person instruction and which ones work best for online learning. For example, if you are conducting an in-person mini-lesson on the key features of a grammatical concept or writing strategy, you'll want to select resources and tactics aligned with that implementation strategy. If students are participating in remote learning when discussing the importance of a focal strategy to a published text, you'll want to organize that activity in ways that correspond with the characteristics of remote learning.

(Continued)

Instructional Modality	Key Suggestions to Consider
Hyflex	We believe that strong hyflex writing instruction keeps in mind the components of this unique instructional modality. Since hyflex instruction calls for some students to join the class online at the same time that others are present in person, we encourage you to incorporate both groups into your writing instruction. When you're conducting direct instruction through the form of a mini-lesson or mentor text explanation, we suggest doing so in a way that is accessible to students in the classroom and those joining via Zoom or a similar platform by live broadcasting the lesson and recording it for students joining online. During activities in which students share their insights with each other, we recommend using technological resources such as Google Docs that will allow all students to collaborate and share their ideas in common ways. Similarly, during writing conferences, you can use the same format whether students are present in person or online so that all students will have the same opportunities for interaction with the teacher.

4

Reading Instruction in the Remote Environment

In this chapter, we explore the most effective ways to engage students in reading instruction in remote contexts, identifying important and essential aspects of teaching reading and reflecting on engaging and meaningful ways to apply those instructional principles to remote language arts instruction. As with the ideas we explored in the previous chapter on effective writing instruction, we believe that there are a variety of ways to use the tools of remote learning to implement the practices of effective reading instruction. In this chapter, we examine key aspects of strong remote instruction and share insights to consider when remotely engaging your students in these practices. First, we describe key components of strong remote reading instruction, noting major features and challenges associated with it. Then, we discuss why it's so important to effectively teach reading in remote contexts, which we follow with an instructional snapshot section that provides an example of Taylor's work with her students. Afterward, we share recommendations for teachers to consider when teaching reading remotely. Finally, we discuss how the ideas in this chapter can be implemented in a range of modalities.

What Are the Key Aspects of Remote Reading Instruction?

The 2019 National Council of Teachers of English (NCTE) policy statement *The Act of Reading: Instructional Foundations and Policy Guidelines* focuses on the many factors that inform reading and instruction, noting that "effective reading instruction acknowledges the complexity of reading" (para. 3). In this document, NCTE advocates for instruction that helps readers build background knowledge of topics and language, incorporates reading and thinking aloud, models the use higher-order thinking skills utilized in reading, and values readers' personal and cultural lenses. We believe that these instructional components can be effectively implemented in remote learning through carefully designed instructional activities that teachers use with their students before they read texts, during the time they spend reading those works, and after they engage with those texts. Laura Robb (2003) describes the merits of reading instruction that focuses on what students do before, during, and after learning by asserting that it helps students:

◆ Enlarge their prior knowledge before learning.
◆ Develop new ways to monitor and improve their comprehension while learning.
◆ Apply new information to meaningful experiences after learning.

In this section, we discuss key components of before-, during-, and after-reading instructional activities and offer our insights on ways each of these components can be connected to remote learning.

Before Reading
As students prepare to read a text, we teachers can take a number of important instructional steps that maximize students' likelihood of success once they begin reading. For example, the 2019 NCTE policy statement *The Act of Reading*, in its Recommendations for Teaching Reading section, calls for teachers to "help students build background knowledge of topics and language that enables students to understand what they read" and to model the use of reading strategies they can use as they read and make sense of a text. By building students' background knowledge of topics and language, as well as demonstrating key strategies that students can use while reading a text, we can position our students to develop strong understandings of the works they read.

Connecting the Before-Reading Stage to Remote Learning
The features and tools of remote learning provide a number of ways for us to conduct engaging and meaningful before-reading activities with our students. For example, we can conduct video mini-lessons dedicated to topics and information that will help students make sense of what they will read. We can share these video resources with students through a variety of formats: if

we are teaching synchronously, we can conduct them in real time through a feature like Zoom or Google Meet. If our students are engaging in asynchronous instruction, we can create videos that we post to a learning management system like Canvas or Blackboard for students to access. In addition, we can use these same kinds of video features to conduct remote read- and think-alouds that we can share with our students. Read- and think-alouds allow us language arts teachers to model effective reading, as well as the use of comprehension and interpretation, strategies that our students can apply to their own works. By sharing these examples remotely, we can provide our students with important aspects of prereading instruction.

Finally, we can use the tools of remote learning to activate students' prior knowledge about topics addressed in the books they're reading. Students can use Google Docs, for example, to write reflections on key issues in a text, which can help them think about information they already know about the topic and establish an accessible point of entry into the work. The activities described here can be conducted through the use of a variety of remote learning tools; while some specific resources will certainly vary based on context, it is essential that we use the features of remote learning to engage our students in meaningful prereading work.

During Reading

While our students read, we educators can help them engage in a number of activities that support their abilities to understand and make meaning of texts. One way to help students interact with the works they read in meaningful ways is to emphasize and value students' unique responses to those pieces, as reading experiences are not just based on the content of a text but also on what ideas and backgrounds individual readers bring to a text (Rosenblatt, 1978). Because of this, we can ask students to make meaningful connections when they read, relating components of texts with their lives, ideas, and experiences. In addition, we can facilitate our students' during-reading success by helping them understand comprehension strategies they can apply while they read (Harvey & Goudvis, 2017). By helping students understand what reading strategies are, why they're important, and how to use them, we can provide them with tactics to use when reading to help them comprehend texts (Robb, 2003).

Connecting the During-Reading Stage to Remote Learning

Remote instruction provides a variety of ways for students to share the connections they make to a text, privileging the individualized and reader-centered approaches that Rosenblatt (1978) describes. Students can use remote learning tools to note what stands out to them about the works they read and how the ideas and information in them connect to their experiences and ideas. We recommend varying the specific instructional tools you use for these connection-based activities based on the nature of the activities and the resources that you feel are best aligned with what you want your students to do. For example, when students make personal connections to a text, they can respond using tools that facilitate the types of connections they're being asked to make: shorter, more immediate responses could be shared through quick-access features like the Zoom chat box, while longer statements can be better fits for reflections shared Google Docs, discussion threads, or posts on learning platforms like Seesaw.

Similarly, students can use the features of remote learning to show how they can apply their knowledge of reading strategies. When utilizing reading strategies like asking questions about a text, creating predictions, or making inferences, students can share their uses through remote learning tools. For instance, if students are making predictions about a text based on a section of a story, they can use Google Docs to share with their classmates and the teacher the predictions they've generated and the texts they feel supports it. We teachers can then examine students' responses and provide them with individualized praise and support based on students' responses. In addition, students can use remote learning tools to document their ongoing interpretations: they can keep online reading journals through Google Classroom, Seesaw, or similar platforms in which they keep track of the inferences they make about characters throughout their experiences reading the piece.

After Reading

After students read a text, we educators can create opportunities for them to take the connections, responses, and interpretations they've developed and use those insights to connect the text to big-picture issues in the world around them. For example, students could relate issues in a text of justice, acceptance, or overcoming obstacles to the ways they see those concepts represented in other situations. This practice helps students see the texts they read as not just school-specific activities but also opportunities to reflect on key ideas and concepts that are relevant to society in a number of ways. The NCTE/International Reading Association Standards for the English Language Arts (1996) assert, in its Guiding Visions section, that students need experiences in English language arts instruction that will allow them "to participate fully as informed, productive members of society." By asking our students to explore how issues and ideas addressed in a text connect to topics and issues in the world around them, we teachers can help our students achieve this meaningful instructional objective. The after-reading stage of reading instruction is a perfect time to do so.

Connecting the After-Reading Stage to Remote Learning

We English language arts teachers can utilize the features and attributes of remote instruction to create ways for our students to relate ideas in texts they read to the world around them. Since the after-reading stage of reading instruction provides opportunities for students to think about societal issues connected to concepts in the works they read, it aligns perfectly with the great deal of online information to which students have access during remote instruction. We educators can create opportunities for students to research real-world events, issues, and people (while identifying credible sources) and connect them to important topics and issues in the works they've read. For example, students could think about the ways characters in a book face prejudice and compare it to similar issues and related events in society today. Through these kinds of activities, students can reflect on and research issues that matter to them while considering the ways that texts provide ways for readers to consider not only the events and issues in a specific work but also what takes place in the world around us.

Why Is It Important?

While there have certainly been many changes made to teaching and learning during the COVID-19 era and the corresponding increase in remote teaching and learning, one aspect of language arts instruction that we believe should continue is the thought-provoking and multifaceted reading instruction that helps students succeed. By providing students with opportunities to build background knowledge, learn reading strategies, make personal connections to a text, and apply textual information to societal issues, we can ensure that students in remote contexts can still engage in high-quality reading instruction.

The benefits of strong reading and literature instruction are significant and numerous; the NCTE's (2019) policy statement *The Act of Reading*, in its Guidelines for Policymakers section, explains that "reading promotes knowledge acquisition and vicarious journeys, encouraging exploration of multiple experiences, plot lines, points of view, and interpretations that enhance the knowledge bases of readers, tying together meaning through their personal and cultural lenses." This statement illustrates the personal, academic, and societal benefits associated with effective reading instruction. By creating instructional opportunities for our students to meaningfully engage with a variety of texts and have engaging, meaningful, and multifaceted experiences with those works, we can provide them with instruction that will benefit them in a variety of ways throughout their lives. Conducting effective reading instruction in the context of remote learning has challenging aspects, but we strongly believe that effective instruction using the practices and ideas discussed in this chapter is valuable and worth the time and effort.

Now, let's take a look at an example of Taylor's work with her students as she engages them in remote reading instruction.

Instructional Snapshot: An Example From Taylor's Work

Remote reading instruction is probably one of my favorite parts of remote instruction because I think it's something I am able to keep "normal" for the students. But I can enhance our virtual instruction with virtual tools available to us. One of the most important parts of remote reading instruction and keeping it "normal" is trying to read actual books to the kids over your video-conferencing tool. YouTube is a great tool, but the value of hearing a teacher read is quite important to young readers.

The most successful lessons I have are when I use Padlet. Padlet is an online tool that allows students to post "sticky notes" and write their own comments. This posts as a message board I can keep up and share with the rest of the class. Recently, we read a book called *Star of Fear*, *Star of Hope*, by Jo Hoestlandt, and we used Padlet to help with our questioning comprehension strategy. Before reading, the students looked at the cover of the book and asked any questions they had. They would log in (so that I knew who posted the question), title the note "Before," write their question(s), and change the color of the sticky note to blue, so that we knew all the blue notes were BEFORE questions. They would do the same thing but label it "Prediction," change the color to pink, and write a prediction.

I read the book beforehand and came up with a predetermined spot to stop at to ask them to post a DURING question. Students tend to struggle with the "DURING" questions, so I often give them stems to help them think deeper than "What will happen at the end?" They posted these questions, and then we finished the story. Before I asked any of my normal post-reading questions, I had them post their "AFTER" questions. Since this book was about people who were Jewish in World War II, the students had a lot of questions about context. I encouraged the students who posted these kinds of questions to come up with a second, deeper question to post.

Instead of jumping in to answer these questions, I allowed the students to answer some questions for their peers. Some students had more schema about World War II and were able to answer questions for the students who asked context-based questions. We had great conversations about the inferential questions some of the other students posted.

It's critical to not only make do with what you have available to you as a teacher but to also use things that you know are going to work well for your students. I miss the feeling of reading a book in front of 20 pairs of wonderful eyes, but with these resources, reading instruction still feels a bit "normal."

Key Recommendations

In this section, we discuss key recommendations to keep in mind when engaging your students in remote reading instruction. These suggestions are designed to help you implement important and beneficial practices of reading instruction in the context of remote learning. They provide insights into ways to apply important aspects of before-, during-, and after-reading to remote instruction:

- ◆ Conduct remote mini-lessons that build key background knowledge and skills.
- ◆ Use the tools of remote learning to share read-alouds and think-alouds with your students.
- ◆ Create remote opportunities for students to activate their prior knowledge before reading.
- ◆ During reading, construct ways for students to remotely share their personal connections and uses of reading strategies.
- ◆ Use the tools of remote learning to help students relate key ideas in the texts they read to the world around them.

By incorporating these suggestions, you'll provide your students with supportive and engaging reading instruction that helps them succeed by maximizing the features of remote teaching and learning. Now, we explore these recommendations in more depth, describing their attributes and ways to put them into action in remote contexts.

Recommendation One: Conduct Remote Video Mini-Lessons That Build Key Background Knowledge and Skills

An effective way to begin this instructional process is by conducting video mini-lessons that will prepare students for reading success by building background knowledge, skills, and strategies that will help them have effective reading experiences. As explained earlier in this chapter, these video mini-lessons can take a range of forms depending on the instructional modality

A Key Aspect of Background Knowledge You'll Focus on Building in Your Mini-Lesson	Key Vocabulary You'll Pre-Teach in Your Mini Lesson	Key Reading Strategies You'll Address in Your Mini-Lesson

Figure 4.1 Mini-Lesson Identification Chart

in which you teach: synchronous instruction aligns with real-time mini-lessons, while asynchronous instruction connects well with videos that you record and share with your students. Regardless of the modality, these video mini-lessons are important and useful ways to share with students important information from which they will draw in their reading.

We recommend identifying background knowledge, vocabulary, and reading strategies that you feel are especially significant to students' abilities to have successful experiences reading a particular text. These selections will be specific to the unique features of the text and to your students' learning needs at a specific time in the school year. (You can use the chart depicted in Figure 4.1 and in Appendix A to identify key aspects of background knowledge, vocabulary, and reading strategies you'll feature in your video lessons.) Once you've identified the key concepts you'd like to address in the lessons, we recommend conducting separate brief mini-lessons of approximately three to five minutes that describe this information. By creating and sharing these video mini-lessons, you can prepare your students to successfully navigate their reading experiences.

Recommendation Two: Use the Tools of Remote Learning to Share Read-Alouds and Think-Alouds With Your Students

Next, we recommend providing students with videos in which you read aloud from one or more texts and model related think-alouds for them. This instructional step follows from the previous one: once we teachers have shared with students mini-lessons that pre-teach key concepts, ideas, and strategies that will facilitate their reading success, we can provide them with video read- and think-alouds that show how expert readers navigate texts. In these read- and think-aloud videos, we can model for students a proficient reading of a text and demonstrate how expert readers think through texts as they read them. These videos are especially useful ways to elaborate on key ideas in the mini-lessons, such as how readers draw on prior knowledge and use key strategies to determine word meanings and interpret a text.

Like with the mini-lesson videos described in the previous recommendation, these read-aloud and think-aloud videos can be shared with students in a range of ways depending on particular instructional modalities. Those of us who teach in a fully synchronous remote context can share these videos with students live through an online meeting platform, while those who teach in asynchronous ways can record the videos and provide students with access to them. When planning these instructional videos, we recommend selecting a text that will engage your students, is on their general instructional level, and will align well with the reading and thinking strategies you want to demonstrate to your students. Once you've selected the text, we recommend identifying specific places in a text where you will think aloud about key strategies, such as how you draw on your prior knowledge when reading about a situation, the ways you determine the meaning of certain vocabulary terms, and how you make inferences and ask questions while you read. After that, you can prepare a brief read- and think-aloud in which you read from the text and model your thought process. By sharing these video resources with students, you can demonstrate for them how to navigate a text; this practice provides remote students with important instructional supports that will help them succeed.

Recommendation Three: Create Remote Opportunities for Students to Activate Their Prior Knowledge Before Reading

Once you've shared the mini-lessons and read- and think-aloud videos described in the first two recommendations, we recommend following these resources with remote opportunities for students to activate their prior knowledge about key issues in texts. To do this, we suggest providing students with ways to reflect on important topics in the texts they'll be reading. These activities, which activate students' prior knowledge and create accessible points of entry that allow them to reflect on key concepts in a text, are well suited for remote learning. Through remote learning, students can share their initial responses on and connections to key themes in a text in a variety of ways, such as chat features, breakout groups, and longer written responses. Students can even use all of these remote learning features when reflecting on the same issue. For example, if students are reading a book with the theme "Acceptance," they might first share their initial thoughts on that concept in the chat box. Then, if technology allows, they could further elaborate on those opening responses by discussing the ideas with peers in breakout groups. Sharing these ideas with peers and further elaborating on them can help students develop their insights even more, which will help them prepare even more to consider the concept in the text they read. Finally, students use the ideas, connections, and insights they've generated through this process to craft longer written responses through Google Docs, discussion board posts, or other remote learning tools that align with more detailed and developed responses.

This series of learning activities can be adapted and implemented in a variety of ways based on particular instructional modalities and learning resources you have available. While some specific components may differ for a range of reasons, we encourage you to use the tools of remote learning to provide your students with a variety of ways to consider and reflect on key issues in a text before reading it. The chart depicted in Figure 4.2 is one that

The Text You're Teaching	A Key Issue in the Text	Why Understanding This Issue Will Benefit Students	Some Activities You'll Use to Help Students Engage With This Issue

Figure 4.2 Key Issues Planning Chart

Sean has used when helping teachers design learning activities based on students reflecting on key issues in texts before reading those works. This chart, which is meant to be a tool to guide your instructional planning, asks you to identify the text you're teaching, a key issue in the text, why you believe understanding that issue is important to students' experiences with the text, and some activities you'll use to help students engage with that issue. You can use this chart repeatedly as you identify key issues and plan learning activities associated with various texts you teach.

Recommendation Four: During Reading, Construct Ways for Students to Remotely Share Their Personal Connections and Uses of Reading Strategies

After students have used the tools and features of remote learning to activate their prior knowledge about key themes and issues in a work of literature, we recommend focusing on students' during-reading experiences. One way to create meaningful reading experiences for students is to construct opportunities for them to make personal connections to a text while reading. This practice is informed by Louise Rosenblatt's (1968) seminal piece *Literature as Exploration*, in which she describes the individualized process that readers experience when making sense of a text. According to Rosenblatt, texts do not have meaning on their own—the meaning of a piece for an individual reader is created through that reader's experience interacting with the text. These interactions can be informed by the personal connections that we readers make when reading a text, highlighting the individualized nature of reading. In addition to making these connections, students can self-monitor their uses of key reading strategies while making sense of the pieces they read. This practice engages students in active reading, helping them monitor their comprehension and reflect on the tactics and strategies they are using to facilitate their understandings of the texts (Harvey & Goudvis, 2017; Robb, 2003).

We feel that these during-reading activities are especially important during remote learning, as they help engage and support students in a situation when learning can be especially difficult for some students. There is a range of ways to facilitate students' personal connections to texts and help them monitor the strategies they use while they read. When creating ways for students to make connections, we suggest utilizing a range of remote learning tools that align with the specific types of connections students are being asked to make. For example, students might make shorter, more immediate connections in a chat box comment and share longer, more developed responses in a breakout group, on a Google Doc, or on a discussion board. Similarly, when you ask students to reflect on and document their uses of reading strategies, we recommend using remote learning tools that match up with the strategies they are using and how they are sharing them. For instance, a shorter and more immediate strategy connection like a summary of a key scene or an observation of something a character does that was surprising could be shared in a chat box or whole-class discussion, while a more in-depth response could be shared through a remote learning tool aligned with that type of reaction. Online reading journals that students keep through the use of remote learning platforms can provide students with opportunities to reflect in more detail about their strategy use and monitor how they use those strategies as they continue to read the text.

Recommendation Five: Use the Tools of Remote Learning to Help Students Relate Key Ideas in the Texts They Read to the World Around Them

The tools of remote learning can play important roles in instructional activities that ask students to relate key ideas in works they read to important issues in the larger world. To do this, we recommend creating opportunities for students to conduct research on issues that they identified in the text and are relevant to them. For example, students can identify and reflect on key ideas, issues, and concepts that they noticed in a literary work and then research world events that are also representative of these ideas. These research-based activities align well with the features of remote learning. As students work independently on high-interest, relevant topics connected to issues in the books they read, we can support them by conducting remote mini-lessons about research-related topics such as finding credible sources, identifying key points, and synthesizing information. We can then remotely confer and check in with them as they do this, noting their progress and providing individualized research and writing suggestions.

We can also use the features of remote learning to create opportunities for students to share the results of their research. By creating opportunities for students to use digital resources to express their insights with an audience other than the teacher, we can add to the authenticity of their work and potentially increase their motivation (Ruday, 2016). Students can share their works with classmates by posting their research and connections to a class-wide discussion board on a learning management system such as Google Classroom, Canvas, or Seesaw. We teachers can use these electronic learning management features to have remote publishing celebrations in which students read one another's works, identifying strengths they notice and making connections between their insights and their peers. These opportunities to share work remotely with an authentic audience can maximize students writing and research experiences.

Adapting for a Range of Modalities

An important topic to consider in a discussion of remote reading instruction is the varying modalities in which remote teaching takes place and the ways to best adapt the best practices of remote literature instruction to these modalities. With this variation in mind, this section describes ideas to consider when implementing the chapter's insights on remote reading instruction across a range of modalities. In it, we describe insights to consider when implementing the chapter's points about effective literature instruction in a range of modes: entirely remote instruction (in which instruction is completely virtual), hybrid instruction (in which students are physically present in the classroom some days and engage through virtual learning other days), and hyflex instruction (in which some students are physically present in the classroom and other students join at the same time virtually). The modality adaptations discussed here are designed to provide you with additional support and recommendations as you engage your students in meaningful and thought-provoking reading instruction.

Instructional Modality	Key Suggestions to Consider
Entirely remote	Teaching reading in an entirely remote way lends itself to the use of a range of technological tools and resources that we teachers can use when engaging students in before-reading, during-reading, and after-reading activities. However, just because there are a variety of tools available does not mean that we should necessarily use every single one. We recommend that you reflect on the technological resources with which you and your students are comfortable and that best align with the instructional goals associated with each activity. For example, the technological tools and innovations used when students make initial connections to key issues in a text or develop personal connections to concepts in the book will differ from those you use when you conduct remote read-alouds and think-alouds or mini-lessons designed to build key background knowledge. We encourage you to think first about the learning goal of each activity and then select the technological tool that you feel will best help you and your students work together to achieve that goal.

(Continued)

Instructional Modality	Key Suggestions to Consider
Hybrid	We feel that the most effective hybrid reading instruction is based on the idea that planning decisions should correspond with the ways students are participating in class on particular days. Since students engaging in hybrid instruction participate in virtual learning on some days and in-person classes on others, we recommend that you reflect on which instructional practices and technological tools would work best with in-person instruction and which ones work best for online learning. When applying this idea specifically to literature instruction, you might consider how students are participating on a particular day (either in person or virtually) and how to best facilitate student learning in that form of participation. For example, if your students are learning in person on a day when they are making personal connections to a text they read, you can construct activities that align with in-person interactions, such as students writing ideas in a response journal and then verbally sharing them with others in the classroom. In contrast, if students are learning virtually on another day, you can select activities that are more aligned with virtual participation. For instance, if students are working on activating their prior knowledge on a virtual learning day, you can create opportunities for them to use remote learning tools to reflect on and share their perspectives on issues in a text before they begin reading it.
Hyflex	The best hyflex reading instruction is designed in ways that incorporate the components of this multifaceted modality, which calls for some students to join the class online at the same time that others are present in person. When teaching reading in a hyflex way, we recommend incorporating both groups simultaneously. For example, if students are sharing personal connections to a text, all students could express their ideas in the same Google Doc or discussion board whether they are joining the class virtually or in person. This would allow all students to participate and share their responses in a common way. If you are conducting a mini-lesson designed to build

Instructional Modality	Key Suggestions to Consider
	students' background knowledge and skills, we suggest identifying ways that will allow for all students to access the information at the same time, such as broadcasting the explanation on Zoom or a similar platform for students joining virtually while also sharing it with the in-person students. You could also record the mini-lesson so that students joining online can be able to access it in the event of technical challenges that might limit their abilities to livestream the content.

5

Culturally Relevant and Sustaining Teaching and Learning in Remote Contexts

In this chapter, we reflect on the best practices for implementing culturally relevant (Ladson-Billings, 1995) and culturally sustaining pedagogy (Paris, 2012) in remote language arts instruction. As we discuss in this chapter, culturally relevant and culturally sustaining instructional practices are essential to all language arts instruction and can be effectively utilized in remote learning to provide teaching and learning activities that center students' identities and experiences. Through the information in this chapter, we discuss key characteristics of culturally relevant and sustaining teaching and provide suggestions to consider when putting these ideas into action in remote instruction. First, we explore important aspects of culturally relevant and sustaining pedagogy, focusing on how it can be connected to remote language arts instruction. Then, we reflect on why it's so important to implement culturally relevant and sustaining instruction in remote contexts. We follow this information with an instructional snapshot section that provides an example of Taylor's work with her elementary school students. Then, we share key recommendations for teachers to consider when putting culturally relevant and sustaining language arts instruction in action. Finally, we discuss how the ideas in this chapter can be implemented in a range of modalities.

What Are the Key Aspects of Remote Culturally Relevant and Sustaining Language Arts Instruction?

Let's begin our exploration of remote culturally relevant and sustaining language arts instruction by considering the fundamental components of these concepts. In her seminal article "But That's Just Good Teaching! The Case for Culturally Relevant Pedagogy," Gloria Ladson-Billings (1995) explains that

> [c]ulturally relevant pedagogy rests on three criteria or propositions: (a) Students must experience academic success; (b) students must develop and/or maintain cultural competence; and (c) students must develop a critical consciousness through which they challenge the status quo of the current social order.
>
> (p. 160)

Instructional practices that incorporate these three criteria can take a number of forms. Ladson-Billings shares that the teachers she studied who implemented culturally relevant teaching not only used a variety of strategies and methods but also had a number of important aspects in common: they felt invested in the communities in which they taught, strongly believed that all students could succeed, and centered students in the curriculum through "fluid and equitable" relationships that created space for students to share their ideas and perspectives in the classroom (p. 163).

Django Paris, in his (2012) piece "Culturally Sustaining Pedagogy: A Needed Change in Stance, Terminology, and Practice," builds off Ladson-Billings's (1995) work and suggests shifting the phrasing and practice from "culturally relevant" to "culturally sustaining," asserting that pedagogy that effectively centers students will work toward sustaining their cultures and identities:

> The term culturally sustaining requires that our pedagogies be more than responsive of or relevant to the cultural experiences and practices of young people—it requires that they support young people in sustaining the cultural and linguistic competence of their communities while simultaneously offering access to dominant cultural competence.
>
> (p. 95)

Instruction that is culturally relevant and culturally sustaining is characterized by instructional practices that value and center students' identities, which helps create opportunities for students' academic success. We can make our classroom culturally sustaining by providing students with opportunities to make authentic connections between academic concepts they learn in school and aspects of their out-of-school lives. In language arts instruction, students can apply their knowledge of reading strategies, writing tactics, and word-study components to texts with which they authentically interact in their cultures, communities, and lived experiences.

We've found that the features of remote language arts instruction and culturally sustaining pedagogies align very well: students can connect key concepts, strategies, and ideas they learn about in their instruction to texts with which they authentically interact in their out-of-school lives. For example, in an instructional sequence focused on figurative language, a teacher can use the principles of culturally relevant and sustaining pedagogy to center students' identities and experiences by constructing opportunities for students to apply this concept to texts they encounter in authentic contexts. In this type of instruction, the teacher could begin by sharing a mini-lesson on figurative language and providing them with a range of examples of its use. After that, the students could reflect on the importance of figurative language and the reasons authors use it in their works. After that, students can identify examples of figurative language they encounter in their out-of-school lives and share them with their classmates using the tools of remote learning. Instructional practices such as this center students' unique experiences and prioritize the forms of literacy with which they engage in out-of-school environments (Duncan-Andrade & Morrell, 2005). While this specific example addresses figurative language, we look in this chapter at a variety of specific topics and concepts that can be meaningfully examined using culturally relevant and culturally sustaining pedagogy.

Why Is It Important?

As Ladson-Billings (1995) and Paris (2012) describe, culturally relevant and culturally sustaining pedagogy is essential to creating equitable learning experiences for students. Similarly, Duncan-Andrade and Morrell (2005) advocate for instructional practices that facilitate authentic connections to students' lives. These ideas are integral to equity-minded instruction in all contexts. Related specifically to remote language arts instruction, the features and principles of culturally relevant and sustaining pedagogy are essential concepts for teachers to consider when organizing remote learning experiences for their students. Since culturally relevant and sustaining pedagogy centers students in the curriculum and values their cultures and identities in the ways that Ladson-Billings (1995) and Paris (2012) describe, it presents a natural connection to the aspects and affordances of remote learning, in which students are not bound by the traditional structures and spaces of school in ways they previously were. In traditional schooling, students leave their homes to enter a distinct physical place. By contrast, in remote learning, students typically are engaging in at least some of their academic work from their homes. (The specific amount of time students spend at home depends on details such as whether they are learning entirely online or in hybrid or hyflex formats.)

We feel that the opportunities remote learning presents for students to learn outside of school creates outstanding connections to culturally relevant and sustaining pedagogy: because students are physically in their communities while they learn, we as educators can create additional opportunities for students' communities and their associated interests, cultures, and backgrounds to incorporate into our instruction. Jamila Lyiscott (2019) calls for educators to create space for students by recognizing and valuing their realities, perspectives, and identities. Through remote learning, we can create these spaces and opportunities by asking students to use the features of remote instruction to facilitate authentic connections between texts with which students interact in their out-of-school lives and the concepts they study in school.

Now, let's take a look at an example of Taylor's work with her students as she applies ideas of culturally relevant and sustaining pedagogy to her remote language arts instruction.

Instructional Snapshot: An Example From Taylor's Work

When choosing texts for any instruction, it is incredibly important to choose texts that are culturally relevant. Thankfully, the curriculum and stories that are given to me tend to already have lots of culturally relevant books included—but we are not all so lucky! Even with these resources, I still find myself outsourcing for great culturally relevant texts. One of my absolute favorite culturally relevant texts is a holiday staple for my classroom: *Hershel and the Hanukkah Goblins*, by Eric Kimmel and illustrated by Trina Schart Hyman. Although I, and many of my students, celebrate Christmas, I enjoy reading and sharing this story each year.

This tradition started when my high school Teachers for Tomorrow teacher, Mrs. Free, read it to us, changing her voice for each of the goblins and making all of us laugh. This memory is still one of my favorites from my K–12 experience. Each year, I take this time to read the book, changing my voice as well, and we discuss the true meaning of the holiday season.

I start off the lesson by asking students what they know about Hanukkah and have them share those things with the class. Usually, they know about the fun Hanukkah traditions, but rarely do they ever know what people who are Jewish are actually celebrating during this time. I proceed to read the book and follow the standard of whatever I'm teaching at the time (character traits, predictions, inferences, etc.)—thankfully, literature is malleable and can be used to teach just about anything! Unfortunately, through Zoom, I am unable to hear the kids' laughs when they hear the newest goblin voice, but I do get some comments saying "lol" in the chat box and I can see their huge smiles on the camera.

After the story, *Hershel and the Hanukkah Goblins* has a summary of Hanukkah's history, and I read that to give the students a background of the holiday. Usually, if we are in person, we play Hanukkah games and do other fun, hands-on activities. Since we were virtual in 2020, and because I have been working on making sure I am being culturally sensitive and accurate, I worked to make sure that this lesson was more meaningful than "Hanukkah is a fun Jewish holiday." I asked my students to ask questions they still had about Hanukkah after the story: "Why were the Jewish people treated badly?" "Why were they fleeing?" "What does Hanukkah mean to Jewish people today?" When they gave me a question, they were able to then go off and do a little research on the question and then post what they learned in a discussion post.

In contrast to the dreidel playing we usually do this day, the students were left with a more meaningful and intentional feeling from this lesson. We ended the day in our closing meeting talking about why people celebrate holidays, and just about every student said something along the lines of being together with the people who mean most to you. In order to wrap the day up, I told them that it's important to remember that each person has a different way of celebrating the holiday season and that spending time together with family may look different for each family, but we all want the same fuzzy feeling.

Key Recommendations

In this section, we share and describe important recommendations for implementing culturally relevant and sustaining pedagogy in remote language arts instruction. These suggestions are designed to help you incorporate essential aspects of Ladson-Billings's (1995) and Paris's (2012) concepts of culturally relevant and sustaining pedagogy in your instruction while also considering the aspects of and opportunities associated with remote learning. The recommendations are designed to center students' authentic experiences and perspectives in remote language arts instruction, creating the "fluid and equitable" instruction that Ladson-Billings (1995, p. 163) describes and the space for students' unique perspectives and identities discussed by Lyiscott (2019).

- ◆ Create video mini-lessons that describe key literacy strategies and provide examples of their authentic, real-world uses.
- ◆ Use the tools of remote learning to engage students in collaborative analyses of the importance of authentically used literacy strategies.
- ◆ Ask students to find real-world examples of literacy strategies and concepts and consider their significance.
- ◆ Provide students with remote opportunities to share the real-world examples they identified and analyzed.

Now, we examine these suggestions in more detail, considering their key features, ways to put them into action, and the ways they center students' individual backgrounds in culturally relevant and sustaining ways.

Recommendation One: Create Video Mini-Lessons That Describe Key Literacy Strategies and Provide Examples of Their Authentic, Real-World Uses

We recommend beginning this instructional process by creating video mini-lessons for students that not only describe key literacy strategies and concepts but also provide examples of the authentic, real-world uses of these concepts. This opening step prepares students for the work they will do as they progress through this sequence by introducing the academic topic on which they will focus and illustrating some ways that concept looks in authentic situations. We educators can use this activity to introduce and discuss any literacy strategy. Figure 5.1 depicts some literacy-related concepts

Writing	Reading	Language Study
• Strong verbs • Specific nouns • Connotation-rich words • Engaging leads • Sensory detail	• Inferences • Connections • Analysis of mood • Predictions • Context clues	• Domain-specific vocabulary relevant to students' authentic experiences • Examples of word roots students encounter in their out-of-school lives

Figure 5.1 Examples of Literacy Concepts and Strategies

Note: Although these are some examples of concepts that we feel can play important roles in effective language arts instruction, we encourage you to select topics that relate to your students' specific needs and the relevant standards for your local context.

and strategies that teachers can describe and connect to authentic, real-world applications and uses.

When constructing a video mini-lesson on a literacy strategy and its authentic uses, we recommend first discussing the concept's essential features by sharing its definition and a few examples related to the students' previous academic work. For example, when discussing the idea of strong verbs, we can talk with students about the attributes of this concept and relate it to examples of strong verbs in a text that students have read that school year. After that, we can connect this concept to authentic, real-world usage by sharing with students examples of strong verbs in a text with which you engage outside of school. For instance, when conducting a mini-lesson on this topic, Sean, an avid sports fan, talked with students about the strong verbs he encounters when watching, listening to, and reading about sports. By doing so, he provided students with examples of this concept he encountered in his out-of-school life. This practice provided a model of real-world application of this writing strategy and worked to show that the class was a place where out-of-school lives and real-world texts are valued. By presenting this information to students through video mini-lessons, we can provide them with resources that they can access repeatedly and are aligned with both synchronous and asynchronous instruction. In addition, the connection between academic concepts and authentic uses that is central to this activity aligns with Ladson-Billings's (1995) statement that culturally relevant teaching must be used to facilitate students' academic success while also creating relevant and culturally affirming instruction.

Recommendation Two: Use the Tools of Remote Learning to Engage Students in Collaborative Analyses of the Importance of Authentically Used Literacy Strategies

Once you've shared with students video mini-lessons that describe and provide authentic examples of literacy strategies, we recommend using the tools of remote learning to create opportunities for students to collaboratively analyze authentically used literacy strategies. To do this, we suggest modeling for students what it looks like to analyze the importance of a literacy strategy used in an authentic, real-world context and then engaging them in collaborative analyses of the importance of that strategy to effective communication and understanding. We recommend beginning this activity by providing students with a video model analysis of a specific concept and then asking them to work collaboratively using remote learning tools to analyze the focal strategy.

For example, after Sean shared examples of strong verbs from broadcasts and articles about sports, he engaged them in a remote activity that asked students to think about why those strong verbs were important to the effectiveness of the works in which they were used. First, he modeled for students his analysis of how one of the strong verbs he identified in the previous activity was important to the effectiveness of the article in which it initially appeared, sharing his insights into why the sportswriter used that verb and how the passage would be different if the author didn't use it. After that, he provided students other examples from the video mini-lesson discussed in step one of this process and asked them to work together in breakout rooms to analyze these examples. Each group analyzed a strong verb example together and shared its thoughts on a Google Slide, providing information about why the author chose to use the concept, its importance to the context in which it was used, and how the piece would be different if it weren't used.

By engaging in this activity, students were able to think about and develop metacognitive understandings of how literacy concepts such as this one are used in authentic ways. While this specific example focuses on strong verbs in sportswriting, this collaborative remote analysis can be applied to all types of real-world applications of literacy strategies. For example, a teacher can model for students how reading strategies such as making connections and constructing inferences can be applied to texts we read in authentic situations as well as how language-study concepts such as identifying word roots and using those roots to interpret word meanings. Regardless of the specific concept being analyzed, students can use remote learning features to engage in collaborative analyses of authentic uses of literacy concepts, which can help them understand how these concepts are used in out-of-school contexts: a skill that they will further develop in the next step of this instructional process.

Recommendation Three: Ask Students to Find Real-World Examples of Literacy Strategies and Concepts and Consider Their Significance

At this stage in the instructional process, students take on increased responsibility and ownership for their learning. In it, students look for authentic, real-world texts that contain or align with the literacy strategy or concept they have been learning about throughout the instructional process. The text that students choose to analyze can be from their lives in any authentic context. By asking students to consider real-world texts with these literacy strategies and concepts in mind, we educators can center students in the curriculum by creating opportunities for them to see connections between these concepts and their everyday lives. This practice aligns with Paris's (2012) statement that culturally sustaining pedagogy privileges cultural and linguistic aspects of students' communities.

When students do this, we teachers ask them to identify examples of a focal concept in any text that represents their authentic interests, experiences, cultures, and/or identities and then reflect on the importance of that concept to the text in which it is located. By doing this, students follow the same cognitive process demonstrated in the first two steps of this instructional process but do so in ways that provide them with more ownership and agency. This activity creates space for students to incorporate into the classroom the texts and topics with which they authentically engage. As we construct these opportunities for students to look for these texts, it's important that we educators value a wide range of texts with which students interact. Emily Machado (2017) asserts that "culturally sustaining pedagogy also encourages us to consider the term 'culture' in a broader sense, including concepts such as popular, youth, and local culture alongside those associated with ethnicity" (para. 2) and identifies a range of ways she and her colleagues have seen students conceptualize culture, such as "Chicago culture, culinary culture, digital culture, and more" (para. 6). By expressing to students that the texts they analyze can take a wide range of forms and focuses, we can work toward constructing student-centered, relevant, and equitable instruction.

This activity connects very well to the features of remote learning: since remote instruction involves students spending more time in their homes and communities and less in the physical environment of school, it facilitates authentic opportunities for students to look at the world around them for examples of focal literacy strategies. For example, students who are focusing on strong verbs in the world around them can consider a range of ways they see, hear, and engage with this concept on an everyday basis in their authentic lives. While students work on this activity, we recommend holding one-on-one conferences with them utilizing remote learning tools. If technology allows, you can hold these conferences with students using individual Zoom breakout rooms. Alternately, students can record their identifications and analyses on Google Docs and you can provide them with questions and suggestions via comments on the documents.

Recommendation Four: Provide Students With Remote Opportunities to Share the Real-World Examples They Identified and Analyzed

Now that students have explored examples of literacy concepts in authentic, real-world texts, it's time for the final step of this instructional process. At this stage, we teachers provide students with remote opportunities to use the features of distance learning in order to share the culturally relevant examples they identified and analyzed. These opportunities to share can take a range of forms. Depending on technological capabilities and available resources, students could create prerecorded presentations that they upload for others to view or they could share synchronous presentations that they share with classmates in real time. However, students can also share their insights in ways they go beyond presentations: they can also create infographics or one-pagers that describe the authentic examples of literacy concepts they identified and analyzed. Whether students give presentations or create documents (or both!), remotely sharing their insights, we recommend ensuring that classmates have opportunities to use the tools of remote learning to comment on what they learned from one another's works. Some great benefits of this activity are how much students can learn about their classmates' identities and how students can share their authentic perspectives with one another.

No matter what specific format you ask students to use when sharing their identifications and analysis (or if you provide them with a range of possible options to use when doing so), an important feature of this stage of the instructional process is that it centers students' unique ideas, insights, and positionalities. By constructing opportunities for students to share real-world connections that value their individual identities, interests, and experiences, we educators are conveying to students that we value the cultures with which our students identify and are committed to creating space in their curriculum for them to share authentic applications of literacy concepts. By doing so, we construct opportunities for students to express their identities and voices (Lyiscott, 2019) and incorporate key principles of culturally relevant (Ladson-Billings, 1995) and culturally sustaining pedagogy (Paris, 2012) in our remote language arts instruction.

Adapting for a Range of Modalities

In this section, we provide ideas to consider when putting this chapter's insights into action in the varying modalities of remote language arts instruction. While the essential attributes of culturally relevant and sustaining pedagogy can be enacted in all modalities, certain aspects of its implementation will vary based on the ways the students are able to interact with the teacher and with one another. Because of this, we share here some ideas to consider when implementing this chapter's ideas about culturally relevant and sustaining language arts instruction in a range of modes: entirely remote instruction (in which instruction is completely virtual), hybrid instruction (in which students are physically present in the classroom some days and engage through virtual learning other days), and hyflex instruction (in which some students are physically present in the classroom and other students join at the same time virtually). The modality adaptations discussed here are designed to provide you with additional support and recommendations as you implement the ideas discussed in this chapter in your instruction.

Instructional Modality	Key Suggestions to Consider
Entirely remote	When engaging students in entirely remote language arts instruction that facilitates authentic connections to their out-of-school lives and interests, you can use a variety of resources and technological tools for students to collaborate, learn, and share. We recommend keeping in mind how each tool aligns with the particular activity in which you are engaging your students. For example, a video mini-lesson you deliver will align with different technological resources than a collaborative activity will. Also, when teaching students remotely, we encourage you to help them capitalize on the fact that they are learning in their homes and communities, which facilitates the kinds of connections between literacy concepts and authentic, real-world texts with which students interact.
Hybrid	An important principle to consider when planning hybrid instruction is that the instructional tools used should align with whether students are learning in person or online. Since students learning in hybrid ways participate in virtual instruction on some days and in-person classes on others, we encourage you to think about how the aspects of culturally relevant and pedagogy align with the specific features of virtual and in-person learning. For instance, if students are working virtually on a day they are working to identify and analyze examples of literacy concepts in their out-of-school lives, you can use the features and attributes of virtual learning to guide them as they do this analysis. Similarly, if students are meeting in person on days they share the authentic examples they found and their analyses of those examples, you'll want to structure the sharing activities in ways that correspond with in-person interaction.

Instructional Modality	Key Suggestions to Consider
Hyflex	Because hyflex teaching involves some students being physically in the classroom at the same time that others join the class online, we recommend thinking about ways that allow both groups to participate in learning activities as effectively as possible. For example, if some students are present in the classroom on a day when students are collaboratively analyzing the importance of a literacy concept to an authentic text and others are joining virtually at the same time, we suggest using technological tools such as Google Slides and Google Docs that allow for students to collaborate and share ideas regardless of their physical location at the time. When students join the class virtually, they can also share authentic examples of real-world texts around them with all the other students in the class, which can further illustrate what real-world applications of concepts can look like and build a learning community that understands and values culturally relevant and sustaining language arts instruction.

6

The Role of Inquiry in Remote Teaching and Learning

In this chapter, we explore the role of inquiry-based teaching and learning in remote language arts instruction. As we discuss in this chapter, inquiry-based language arts instruction is a pedagogical framework that not only privileges students' curiosities and interests (Ruday & Caprino, 2021) but also aligns well with the features of remote learning. In this chapter, we describe what inquiry-based language arts instruction is and share ideas to consider when implementing this instructional approach remotely. First, we examine key aspects of effective inquiry-based remote language arts instruction, which we follow with an exploration of the importance of this pedagogical framework to effective teaching in remote contexts. After that, we look at an instructional snapshot section that provides an example of Taylor's work with her students. Then, we share recommendations for teachers to consider when putting inquiry-based remote language arts instruction into action. Finally, we discuss how the ideas in this chapter can be implemented in a range of modalities.

What Are the Key Aspects of Inquiry-Based Remote Language Arts Instruction?

Inquiry-based pedagogy is a form of teaching and learning that centers around thought-provoking, big-picture, essential questions that students investigate (McTighe & Wiggins, 2013). An essential question is defined as "a question that lies at the heart of a subject or a curriculum (as opposed to either being trivial or leading), and promotes inquiry and uncoverage of a subject" (Wiggins & McTighe, 2005, p. 342). A strong essential question, according to McTighe and Wiggins (2013), should possess all or most of these seven attributes:

◆ is open-ended;
◆ is thought-provoking;
◆ calls for higher-order thinking;
◆ points toward important, transferable ideas;
◆ raises additional questions and sparks further inquiry;
◆ requires support and justification, not just an answer;
◆ and recurs over time, or can be revisited frequently.

(p. 3)

By utilizing essential questions, we language arts teachers can incorporate the features and benefits of inquiry-based learning in our instruction. While essential questions can be applied to a range of subjects, they are especially useful and beneficial in language arts because of the ways they provide opportunities for students to think about relevant and engaging issues that are present across the works with which they interact. The approach therefore "positions *authentic, real-world questions, not specific texts*" in a central role in the curriculum (Ruday & Caprino, 2021, p. 11). By engaging in inquiry-based language arts instruction, students are able to engage with essential questions that facilitate authentic connections with their lives and real-world issues and can draw on their experiences interacting with a wide range of texts as they reflect on and construct their responses to those questions (Ruday & Caprino, 2021).

We feel that inquiry-based language arts instruction is especially aligned with remote teaching and learning. The features of remote learning, such as the opportunities it provides for students to work independently and in self-directed ways, match up very well with the nature of inquiry-based learning. Since this instructional approach prioritizes students' unique experiences, investigating questions and topics that have real-world connections, it lends itself to individualized explorations that can take place through a number of learning modalities and structures. Once students know the essential question they're investigating and have clear understandings of how to conduct an inquiry, they can work remotely on analyzing a range of texts that address that question. While students work on these inquiries remotely, we teachers can support them in a variety of ways. We can use the features of remote learning to provide students with guidance, such as sharing video mini-lessons on important ideas to keep in mind, giving feedback on their work through Google Docs, holding one-on-one conferences with them through Zoom, and constructing ways for students to offer virtual support to each other. Ultimately, once they've completed their inquiries, students can share the results of their investigations through remote presentation tools. Now, we consider why remote inquiry-based language arts is important to effective remote teaching and learning.

Why Is It Important?

Inquiry-based learning can benefit students in a variety of ways: works such as Krebs and Zvi's (2015) *The Genius Hour Guidebook* and Juliani's (2015) *Inquiry and Innovation in the Classroom: Using 20% Time, Genius Hour, and PBL to Drive Student Success* discuss how inquiry-oriented experiences can maximize student engagement and achievement. These benefits are especially applicable to remote instruction, which presents significant challenges for teachers as they work to engage students and help them achieve academic goals. In a 2020 *New York Times* article titled "Students, Parents and Teachers Tell Their Stories of Remote Learning" by Amelia Nierenberg, students reported less motivation and lower academic performance during remote learning.

Inquiry-based instruction is of great importance to remote language arts teaching because the engagement and achievement it facilitates address the key challenges that students in Nierenberg's piece described. By providing students with opportunities to conduct multitextual inquiries that revolve around authentic, real-world essential questions, we can construct learning opportunities for our students that excite them about learning and help enhance academic achievement. Remote language arts instruction is an especially apropos context for experiencing the benefits of inquiry-based learning since the use of essential questions is naturally linked with strong language arts teaching and learning. When we pose essential questions and challenge our students to use a variety of texts in order to respond to those questions, we construct meaningful, relevant, and engaging learning opportunities for our students. By contrast, if we ask our students to read and analyze single, specific works without utilizing essential questions to help them consider important issues in those texts, it would be harder for students to engage in the authentic learning that inquiry-based instruction facilitates. When we construct opportunities for students to examine thought-provoking, engaging, and relevant questions that facilitate higher-order thinking and require complex analysis (McTighe & Wiggins, 2013), we can help our students have engaging and motivating learning experiences in our remote language arts classes.

Now, let's take a look at an example of Taylor's work with the students in her language arts class as she incorporates inquiry-based instruction.

Instructional Snapshot: An Example From Taylor's Work

Inquiry-based instruction is something that we find incredibly important in my classroom, especially while teaching gifted students. Every year, we allow our students to complete a "passion project." These projects are quite the undertaking in person; trying to do it in a remote learning environment is even more stress-inducing. But the value of these projects is evident when the kids beam from joy when sharing what they've learned about.

The beginning of passion projects is always hard. How do fifth-graders (1) think of a topic, (2) think of a question or research stimulus, and (3) think of a final product that is cohesive? One way I help students with their launch is to allow them to do a chart walk around the room and write ideas in different categories: famous people, sports, science, animals, careers, and history. In order to edit this to work virtually, we created a Google Slide presentation that the students will use to still complete a "chart walk" of sorts. What's important here? Remembering that you need to discuss rules and expectations before this lesson to avoid the "He deleted my comment!" or "She copied me!" remarks.

Once we had brainstormed, students would send me a message through Schoology with a proposal for their passion projects. They had to tell me what their topic would be, what question or research stimulus they'd be researching, and three ideas they had for a final project. Once they had an idea I found acceptable (expectations are based on student ability: Are they underestimating themselves? Can they do more? Are they overestimating the amount of work they will need to do in order to answer their question? etc.).

Then, I assigned time during our Daily-5 for them to work on their inquiry. They were given a 15-minute-a-day time limit and a deadline. On Fridays, during their Daily-5 time, since I didn't pull small groups because of our Specials schedule, I allowed them to "sign up" for times to Zoom with me if they had questions or if they were stuck. That allowed them to still have guidance but kept me from being too overbearing in their work. When I hadn't heard much from them, I'd set up a time to pull them aside to make sure they were keeping up.

In a perfect world, I would have time to let them continually work on a passion project—but with the inconsistency of the remote learning environment this can be tough! Dedicating as much time to it and doing your best is really all you can do. Remember how much these kids *LOVE* learning about what they care about, and you'll see the time is worth it!

Key Recommendations

Now, we share important suggestions to consider when incorporating inquiry-based learning in your remote language arts instruction. These recommendations are designed to help you engage and support your students in ways that embody the best practices of inquiry-based teaching and learning while applying this approach to remote contexts. By implementing these suggestions in your instruction, you'll help your students learn using essential questions (Wiggins & McTighe, 2005; McTighe & Wiggins, 2013) and achieve the motivation and engagements benefits of inquiry-based learning (Krebs & Zvi, 2015; Juliani, 2015), which are especially aligned with language arts instruction (Ruday & Caprino, 2021) and are particularly important to the context of remote teaching and learning, in which many students struggle with feeling motivated for and engaged in school (Nierenberg, 2020).

Our four recommendations for implementing inquiry-based remote language arts instruction are as follows:

- Share video mini-lessons that convey the fundamental components of inquiry.
- Use the features of remote learning to help students respond to the texts they read and connect those texts to the inquiry's essential question.
- Provide remote support for students as they synthesize their responses to the unit's essential question.
- Create ways for students to remotely share the results of their inquiries and analyses.

Now, let's think in more detail about these recommendations, specific ways to put them into action, and why they represent effective remote inquiry-based language arts instruction.

Recommendation One: Share Video Mini-Lessons That Convey the Fundamental Components of Inquiry

We recommend beginning the process of remote inquiry-based language arts instruction by creating and sharing with students videos that convey key aspects of inquiry. Depending on the specific nature of your instructional

delivery and your school's remote learning format, these could be prerecorded videos you share or live instruction you conduct. No matter which
format your instruction takes, we recommend providing students with two
short video mini-lessons. In the first one, we suggest talking about inquiry
and essential questions in general, sharing with students the way inquiry
involves using a variety of sources to answer one or more essential questions,
talking with them about the features of essential questions, and providing
them with some examples of inquiry. Then, in the next mini-lesson, we recommend describing the essential question students will investigate in the
inquiry the class will conduct and the texts that will make up that inquiry.
These brief, focused lessons will orient students to the essential aspects
of inquiry-based language arts instruction and prepare them for the work
they'll do throughout the unit as they interpret a variety of texts, synthesize
their key ideas, and use the information in those texts to answer the unit's
essential question.

Recommendation Two: Use the Features of Remote Learning to Help Students Respond to the Texts They Read and Connect Those Texts to the Inquiry's Essential Question

Now that students understand key aspects of inquiry-based language arts
learning, the next step is to engage them in this process by helping them
respond to the texts they encounter in the inquiry. By constructing these
responses, students can interpret the unit's texts and connect them to the
essential question on which this learning process is focused. To maximize
the effectiveness of doing so in remote learning, we recommend reflecting
on the features of remote learning that you believe will best help students
share their responses to the works they read in the inquiry. When constructing these activities, we recommend varying the remote learning tools based
on the types of responses you want students to create. For example, as we've
discussed in previous chapters, if students are sharing brief responses, such
as initial reactions to a text's events or characters, they can do so using tools
that facilitate those kinds of responses, such as a chat box comment. By contrast, when students compose longer, more developed responses, such as
text-based inferences, connections to world events, or detailed discussions of
a character's motivation, we recommend constructing response options that
align with the time and space these responses would take, such as Google
Docs, Zoom breakout group discussions, or online discussion boards.

Since inquiry-based language arts instruction is rooted in students' reflections on essential questions, the most effective remote reading responses in
this context are those that gradually develop students' awareness of key issues
in the texts and provide opportunities for them to connect their insights to the
concepts that the essential question presents. While these specific responses
can take a range of forms, the inquiry's essential questions can establish a

common thread in the ways we ask our students to respond to the texts they encounter. By using the inquiry's essential question as a framework for student responses, we can prepare students for the next stage of this instructional process, in which students work to synthesize their insights about the essential question.

Recommendation Three: Provide Remote Support for Students as They Synthesize Their Responses to the Unit's Essential Question

After students remotely respond to the texts they read as part of this inquiry, the next step is for us as teachers to support them as they synthesize their understandings of those texts and use those insights to help them respond to the essential question. (Students will ultimately share the results of their inquiries and their corresponding analyses in the final step of this instructional process.) To help students synthesize their responses, we recommend providing a range of support opportunities designed to help them as they reflect on the texts they've read and how those texts combine to help them address the essential question. An initial step to help students synthesize their ideas is to provide them with a model of what this kind of analysis looks like. For example, when explaining to students how they'll synthesize their insights, you could share with them how you've done similar work by sharing with them a different essential question that you've investigated and describing how you used a range of texts to address this question. This can be done through the form of a video mini-lesson as described in the initial step of this instructional sequence. By providing students with this information, you'll share with them in an accessible way what the synthesis process looks like and give them a framework that they can then apply to the essential question they're investigating.

After you've shared this model with students and discussed it with them, we recommend using remote learning tools to support students individually as they construct their own interpretations. Depending on the specific nature of your remote instruction, you could support students through one-on-one conferences in Zoom breakout rooms, feedback via Google Docs, recorded voice memos, or other methods of providing students with individualized responses. The best method of support to use is one that aligns with the features of your remote learning context and will be useful and accessible to your students. Regardless of the specific support tactic you utilize, we suggest sharing with students individualized feedback that focuses on the ways they are synthesizing the key ideas from the texts they've examined in ways that address the unit's essential question. As students craft their responses, it's important that they address the essential question in ways that represent their unique perspectives and that they develop their insights with specific evidence from the text. By using these remote learning tools, you can provide students with support as they create and fine-tune these responses and analyses.

Recommendation Four: Create Ways for Students to Remotely Share the Results of Their Inquiries and Analyses

In the final step of this instructional process, students remotely share the results of their inquiries by expressing how they've synthesized the texts they examined in the unit and used them to craft responses to the unit's essential question. These opportunities to share their insights can provide excellent learning experiences for students, as they not only get to share their own analyses and syntheses but also are able to learn from the ways that their classmates responded to the unit's essential questions. The similarities and differences between students' inquiry-based insights can provide excellent opportunities for students to reflect on common threads and to learn from the additional points and ideas their classmates made but they had not.

In order to create ways for students to share these results remotely, we recommend providing them with a range of options that align with the focus of the activity. Like with the out-of-school connections and applications described in Chapter Five, there are a variety of methods students can utilize as they share their inquiry responses. For example, students can construct recorded video presentations that convey their responses to the essential question and the ways the unit's text helped them reach that conclusion. These presentations can be shared synchronously if that aligns with your instructional delivery method or could be recorded and shared asynchronously. Alternately, students can create written responses, infographics, or one-pagers and share them with their classmates synchronously or asynchronously. No matter what kind of product students use to share their ideas and whether their works are shared synchronously or asynchronously, we recommend building in remote opportunities for students to comment on one another's inquiry results by providing compliments on their peers' insights, similarities to their own works, and ways their classmates' ideas helped them consider new ideas. These opportunities to share can emphasize the individualized nature of inquiry, call attention to commonalities, and build a collaborative remote learning community.

Adapting for a Range of Modalities

When implementing these ideas about remote inquiry-based language arts instruction, it's important to consider the range of modalities in which remote learning can take place and make adaptations according to the form that aligns with the context in which you and your students are working. With that in mind, we share in this section ideas to consider when putting this chapter's key ideas about inquiry-based language arts instruction in a variety of modalities: entirely remote instruction (in which instruction is completely virtual), hybrid instruction (in which students are physically present in the classroom some days and engage through virtual learning other days), and hyflex instruction (in which some students are physically present in the classroom and other students join at the same time virtually). These adaptation suggestions are designed to help you best align the principles of inquiry-based literature instruction with specific instructional modalities.

Instructional Modality	Key Suggestions to Consider
Entirely remote	When engaging students in inquiry-based instruction in an entirely remote modality, we recommend reflecting on the remote tools and resources available and selecting those that best align with specific activities. For example, when sharing information with students about the key aspects of inquiry-based learning and the features of essential questions, we suggest using video mini-lessons like those described in the chapter. By contrast, when supporting students as they synthesize their responses to the unit's essential question, we recommend using remote support tools that facilitate your ability to respond to them individually, such as one-on-one conferences through Zoom breakout rooms, feedback using Google Docs, or other similar methods of individual interaction. As you select these specific inquiry-based remote learning activities, we encourage you to think about the features and learning goals of each activity and select implementation forms that will help students most effectively engage with that activity. This intentional selection will help maximize students' inquiry-based learning experiences.

Instructional Modality	Key Suggestions to Consider
Hybrid	To successfully implement inquiry-based learning instruction in a hybrid modality, we recommend focusing on whether students will be learning in person or virtually on specific days and aligning the day's instruction with that modality. Ensuring this alignment will help students engage with and learn from inquiries as effectively as possible. For example, if students are present in person on a day when they respond to an inquiry-based text they're reading, we recommend creating in-class opportunities for them to reflect on their ideas and share verbally with peers, such as reflecting in writing on their ideas and then sharing their thoughts in small-group and whole-class discussions. However, if students are engaging virtually on a day when they respond to the texts they read, we suggest using remote learning tools to provide them with opportunities to respond to the texts they've read and share those insights with classmates. This purposeful selection of learning tools can facilitate student engagement academic success.
Hyflex	To support student inquiry in hyflex instruction, it's important to construct and implement learning activities that engage students who are joining the class online as well as those who are participating in a face-to-face format. The best hyflex inquiry-based instruction, we feel, allows for students to meaningfully engage in inquiry through either one of these formats. To implement inquiry-based language arts instruction in a hyflex modality, we recommend constructing learning activities in which students participating online and those participating face-to-face can meet the learning objective. For example, if the objective of a lesson or activity is for students to understand key aspects of inquiry, you can share a video mini-lesson with students who are participating virtually at the same time that you share it with those who are joining in person. If students are sharing the results of their inquiries, you can construct ways for all students to do so using technological tools that all students can access. For example, if students give presentations on their inquiries, those presentations can

Instructional Modality	Key Suggestions to Consider
	be livestreamed so that all members of the class can learn from their peers and provide feedback. (These presentations can also be recorded so that students who are unable to join the class in real time due to technological challenges or other issues can still see them.) Also, if students create a document about their inquiries such as infographics or one-pagers, they can share them and give feedback to peers via Google Docs so that all students can access those responses whether they engage virtually or in person.

7

Assessing Student Learning

In this chapter, we explore best practices and key ideas to consider related to effective formative and summative assessment in the context of remote language arts instruction. As we discuss further in the chapter, literacy assessment is a complex and nuanced endeavor: if done well, it cannot be easily simplified or based on measures that prioritize efficiency over usefulness and authenticity (International Literacy Association, 2017). In remote teaching and learning, effective assessment takes on a new dimension as we language arts teachers must determine the formative and assessment processes that best guide teaching and learning while also aligning with the features of remote instruction. This chapter addresses these topics in a variety of ways. First, we describe key components of remote language arts assessment, noting what can make these assessments useful and effective. After that, we consider why it's so important to assess students in meaningful and authentic ways in remote contexts. Then, we look at an example of Taylor's assessment-related work with her elementary school students. Next, we share recommendations for teachers to consider when assessing student learning remotely. Finally, we discuss how the information described in this chapter can be adapted to fit with a range of modalities.

What Are the Key Aspects of Remote Language Arts Assessment?

Effective assessment is central to many discussions of effective language arts instruction. The National Council of Teachers of English (2018) and International Literacy Association (2017) recently published policy statements and briefs about the best practices of assessment—both documents addressed the various forms that assessments can take and the need for literacy assessments can be aligned with their particular instructional contexts. The International Literacy Association's (2017) document *Literacy Assessment: What Everyone Needs to Know* discusses "the importance of considering the types of reading and writing being assessed, the assessment's purpose, and the specific students being assessed" (p. 2). Similarly, the National Council of Teachers of English's (2018) position statement *Literacy Assessment: Definitions, Principles, and Practices* asserts that "[l]iteracy assessment is varied and includes multiple measures of different domains, including processes, texts, and reflection" (n.p.).

These ideas about literacy assessment being adapted for specific contexts and purposes are especially relevant to our focus in this book on remote language arts instruction. As we teach in remote contexts, it's important to keep in mind what types of assessment best align with the features and attributes of remote teaching and learning. With this in mind, this section explores best practices of formative and summative assessment that correspond with language arts instruction in remote contexts. Let's begin by examining what strong remote formative assessment in literacy instruction can look like.

Formative Assessment

Formative assessment practices, low-stakes assessment practices designed to gauge students' understanding and therefore drive future instruction, are important to language arts instruction in all teaching and learning formats. In its position statement *Expanding Formative Assessment for Equity and Agency*, the National Council of Teachers of English (2020) explains that formative assessment is "a practice of or commitment to frequently checking for understanding and adjusting instruction" (n.p.). We feel that regular and useful formative assessment practices are especially important to remote instruction, in which communication with students takes a variety of forms and differs from traditional in-class interaction. For example, in a synchronous lesson on Zoom, an asynchronous learning activity, or a hybrid or hyflex class session, it can be challenging for teachers to have a clear understanding of how students are grasping key content. Because of this, we recommend being as intentional and deliberate as possible when utilizing formative assessment in your remote language arts instruction.

In addition to in-class applications of knowledge in which students demonstrate their understandings through remote learning tools such as discussion board posts, breakout group conversations, or comments on Google Docs, we suggest asking students to answer exit questions or complete exit activities at the end of a lesson or learning activity. Students can share their responses to these questions or activities in ways that correspond with your particular remote learning format; for instance, they can share insights in the Zoom chat box, share them on a Google Form or Doc, express them on an online discussion board (such as those in platforms like Google Classroom and Canvas), or through the use of another method that best aligns with the features of the context associated with your instruction. By asking students to complete these responses, you will gain regular formative assessment information that you can use to evaluate your students' understandings and guide your future instruction.

Summative Assessment

We feel that the most effective remote language arts assessment provides students with ways to authentically express and apply the ideas and insights they've gained through their learning experiences. To do this, we teachers can design summative assessments that prioritize the application of knowledge over the recall of information. While authentic application is a key principle of literacy assessment in general (Dolghan, Kelly, & Zelkha, 2010), we believe it is especially important to effective assessment in remote teaching and learning because of the alignment that exists between the features of remote assessment and the opportunities for students to authentically express and apply their knowledge. For example, since students in remote language arts instruction are not spending as much (or any) time in the classroom, we can design assessment opportunities in which they are asked to apply knowledge they've gained and concepts they've considered in ways. In contrast, tests and quizzes in which students recall information are not as aligned with the features of remote instruction because they do not create the opportunities for authentic application that students can do in their remote learning time.

Authentic language arts assessments can take a wide range of forms. We recommend providing students with a range of opportunities to demonstrate and apply their knowledge in ways that have applicability to real-world contexts and situations. For example, students could create websites or podcasts on social issues reflected in texts they've read, using the texts as well as other ideas to inform their responses. Similarly, students can write for real-world audiences on topics that matter to them, which will allow the students to not only convey their analyses of those topics but also to apply the writing strategies and grammatical concepts they've studied. Students can even work together to create virtual conferences or webinars in which they identify authentic examples or applications of concepts they've studied—these virtual conferences can be conducted among the students or could be shared with wider audiences, such as caregivers, families, and community members. All these authentic applications are ways that facilitate students' abilities to remotely apply and utilize the information they learn in language arts.

Why Is It Important?

Implementing regular, authentic, and useful assessment is important to strong remote language arts instruction for a variety of reasons. For instance, the use of consistent formative assessment is especially important to remote teaching because of the way it provides teachers with frequent opportunities to evaluate student progress. We feel these regular, low-stakes assessments are of particular significance in remote contexts where teachers and students don't have the same opportunities for one-on-one in-person interaction that traditional face-to-face learning provides. In the face-to-face classroom, for example, it can be easier to check in with students to gauge their understanding or to evaluate in an informal way how well students are grasping key content. By asking students to complete remote exit questions or exit activities, we teachers will gather useful and consistent assessment data that we can use to inform our instruction as we guide students' learning.

In addition to the benefits provided by regular remote formative assessments, it's also important to consider the positive features of authentic remote summative assessments, such as those described in the previous section of this chapter. These opportunities for students to express their understandings of important concepts in ways that align with real-world contexts and situations can increase student motivation by providing opportunities for them to meaningfully apply the information they've learned. Since students have reported lower motivation and academic performance in remote learning (Nierenberg, 2020), engaging and meaningful assessments that mirror real-life applications are especially important in this context. Also, since authentic assessments provide teachers with a great deal of information about how well students are able to apply key concepts and ideas they've learned (Wiggins, 1998), incorporating these types of assessments provides useful information on student learning that can drive future instruction. For example, after we teachers look at the ways students perform on authentic assessment projects and apply key concepts and ideas while doing so, we can use that assessment data to decide on concepts we need to revisit in our future instruction. This connection between summative assessments and future instruction is especially important to remote instruction because it can enhance students' abilities to be academically successful in a potentially challenging learning environment.

Now, let's take a look at Taylor's work with assessment in her remote language arts instruction.

Instructional Snapshot: An Example From Taylor's Work

Assessment has been one of the hardest parts of remote teaching. A lot of my in-person formative assessments were sticky notes or discussions I had with students after the lesson. That is not easy virtually, especially with the inequity of home environments.

Consistently, I use Quizizz to assess my students formatively. Quizizz is a fun quiz generator that allows the students to answer questions while getting "Power-Ups." These are great comprehension assessments, as you can stick in comprehension questions about the book they are reading—or you can set up questions that directly assess the skill you are working on: context clues, predictions, synonyms, and the like. I am able to look at the results of the Quizizzes immediately and then make note of who I need to pull for small-group intervention or what I need to reteach.

For summative assessments, I use GoFormative to assign the district-written tests. These tests allow students to be exposed to the standardized test structure. I do get some data from these tests, but I rely on my formative test data and what I know about the student to create a "grade." Because of inequitable home environments, I cannot assume that these tests are giving me reliable data (whether because I am worried parents are helping or because I am worried they are in loud, busy environments).

When struggling to come up with authentic data for assessments, I came up with an idea. My students love writing; I have maybe two or three who do not enjoy it. When we were wrapping up our last fiction unit, I decided to allow my students to write a story using the important things (the standards) we had learned about from that unit. In particular, we learned about (1) character traits, (2) conflict/resolution, and (3) theme. So the students were urged to write a story with a clear conflict/resolution, where the resolution helped show the theme, with a character that you could clearly visualize. Right away, my students started brainstorming and telling me their ideas. They had a blast writing, and I had a blast reading; I had stories about jungle safaris, aliens, and the *Invasion of the Sour Patch Kids*. Using data from GoFormative and their performance on the story, I was able to figure out who actually understood character traits, who actually understood how conflict interacts with resolution, and how that resolution can teach a lesson. I really was able to see who knew the standards and who just picked an answer on the test.

Key Recommendations

In this section, we share suggestions to consider when implementing assessment practices in remote language arts instruction. These recommendations reflect key principles of effective assessment that align with the features and attributes of remote teaching and learning; they are designed to help you put the ideas discussed in this chapter into action in your own remote instruction. They will guide you as you implement context-specific assessment (International Literacy Association, 2017; National Council of Teachers of English, 2018) through thoughtful formative (National Council of Teachers of English, 2020) and authentic summative assessment (Dolghan et al., 2010). Specifically, we recommend the following four guidelines when assessing student knowledge in remote learning:

◆ Construct formative assessments aligned with the features of remote learning.
◆ Use remote formative assessments throughout instructional activities and as closure to those activities.
◆ Provide a range of remote-friendly, authentic summative assessment options.
◆ Ensure alignment between the summative authentic assessment options and key learning objectives.

Now, let's look at each of these recommendations individually by examining what each one can look like in action and why it represents a key component of remote language arts assessment.

Recommendation One: Construct Formative Assessments Aligned With the Features of Remote Learning

The first recommendation we have for assessing students' remote language arts learning is to create formative assessments that are aligned with features of remote learning. To construct these assessments, we teachers need to think strategically about two questions: (1) Do these formative assessment tools work well with the remote learning format in which we're teaching? and (2) Do these assessments provide useful information about student learning progress? If we can answer yes to both of these questions regarding a particular formative assessment tool, then that tool is an effective one to use. For example, if we're teaching a synchronous class in which all students are participating remotely Zoom, then an effective formative assessment could be for all students to answer a question at the end of class that corresponds with a lesson's key learning goals and share their responses to that question in the Zoom chat box. This type of response corresponds with these questions because it aligns with that particular method of remote instruction and provides the teacher with information about how well students are understanding key content.

Applying this framework to another modality, if a language teacher is teaching a class taught in a hybrid format in which students are learning in school some days and remotely on others, we can craft formative assessments that align with a given day's features. For example, students might share verbal responses on days in which they participate in school but would need to express their ideas remotely on days they learn outside of school. If students are conducting this remote learning asynchronously, they can share ideas on Google Docs or Google Forms that provide the teacher with useful formative assessment data. It's essential that we teachers consider the specific remote learning context and the assessments that best align with that context while providing us with useful information about student learning progress.

Recommendation Two: Use Remote Formative Assessments Throughout Instructional Activities and as Closure to Those Activities

As you put into action the ideas described in Recommendation One about the strategic use of remote formative assessment, we recommend doing so at multiple points in the instructional process. Students can demonstrate their knowledge with formative assessments that can be implemented in the middle of an instructional sequence as well through assessments that are used as closure activities at the end of a class period or learning activity. For example, formative assessments that can be implemented during an instructional process could involve written responses that students share remotely to readings they've done or low-stakes writings that they can share with you through a digital platform. Both of these assessments will provide you with useful information aligned with remote instruction about how well students are understanding key concepts related to their language arts work. We recommend evaluating these formative assessments during the instructional period to the extent possible and then in more depth after class. For instance, if students are completing low-stakes writings in which they apply a certain writing strategy or concept, we suggest giving each piece an overview evaluation during the class time as they submit the pieces and then looking at them in more depth afterward to evaluate student progress and make decisions about what to teach next.

In addition to these in-process formative assessments that students complete in the middle of an instructional sequence, we recommend using low-stakes exit questions and exit activities that students can use to convey their understanding of key concepts and ideas. For example, if students are learning about a particular writing strategy in the day's class, they might answer a question about why authors use that strategy to enhance their works and share their ideas remotely through a format that aligns with the features of your remote teaching and learning. Similarly, if students have focused on analyzing a particular text that day, they can respond to a question that asks them to demonstrate their understanding by commenting on something in that text that especially struck them, connecting the text to another one they've read, or relating the piece to an essential question or big-picture topic. Students can then share these ideas through digital tools such as a Zoom chat box, Google Doc, Google Form, online discussion board, or another resource that aligns with the features of your particular learning context, which will give you quick access to their insights and provide you with useful formative assessment data that can guide your future remote instruction.

Recommendation Three: Provide a Range of Remote-Friendly, Authentic Summative Assessment Options

When implementing summative assessments in remote language arts instruction, we recommend providing students with a range of options to authentically demonstrate their knowledge. As discussed earlier in this chapter, these authentic assessment options can take a range of forms; one especially important aspect of this assessment type is that it gives students opportunities to demonstrate their knowledge through application rather than recall. To make them aligned with remote learning, it's important to reflect on how well specific assessments correspond with the technological tools to which your students have access and will provide them with opportunities to apply their knowledge in meaningful ways. By giving students a range of possible authentic summative assessments from which to choose, we can increase their opportunities for agency and motivation in their academic work.

Figure 7.1 lists and describes some possible authentic summative assessments that we feel can work well in remote teaching and learning. The ideas described in this table are meant to provide useful information on types of assessments that are aligned with remote instruction and the reasons they align with remote instruction.

Assessment	Brief Description	Why It Aligns With Remote Teaching and Learning
Website on social issue	Students can create websites on social issues reflected in texts they've read, using those texts as support.	This assessment format provides students with authentic opportunities for students to share their ideas in ways that are meant to be created remotely for remote audiences, creating a strong alignment with remote instruction.
Podcast on social issue	Similar to the previously described websites, students can create podcasts on social issues in the texts they've read and use those texts to support their ideas.	Podcasts can make outstanding remote assessments because they are meant to be shared remotely and align with both individual and collaborative work. For example, students can create podcasts on their own or they can interview others and remotely incorporate their perspectives.

Figure 7.1 Possible Authentic Summative Assessments

Recommendation Four: Ensure Alignment Between the Summative Authentic Assessment Options and Key Learning Objectives

When we provide students with a range of authentic summative assessment options like those described in the previous recommendation, it's important that we make sure that all the possible assessments are aligned with key learning objectives that we want to ensure students understand. To do this, it's important that we teachers decide on the central concepts that we want students to show their understandings of and select assessments that will allow them to demonstrate those understandings. Application-based authentic assessments align well with this goal, as they provide students with a range of ways to demonstrate key understandings. For example, students could use many of the assessments described in Recommendation Three to demonstrate mastery of essential learning objectives. A key component of this process is to decide on important learning goals that students can show their understanding of in a variety of ways. For instance, students can convey their mastery of an important idea, topic, or concept through a website, a podcast, an infographic, a one-pager, or another format.

When giving students a range of ways to demonstrate their understanding, it's important to convey to them the key objectives that they'll need to show mastery of regardless of the format they select. For instance, if students are examining a societal issue and its relation to texts they've read, we educators can emphasize to them that they'll show their knowledge of this issue and the texts they studied through any assessment option they select. It's a good idea to provide students with a list of key topics or concepts they'll need to show their understanding of, regardless of the summative assessment option they pick. This can ensure consistent assessment and provide you with important information about student learning that can guide your future instruction.

Adapting for a Range of Modalities

When implementing the remote language arts assessment ideas and strategies discussed in this chapter, it's important to reflect on the range of possible modalities and make assessment-related decisions aligned with the ways you and your students are working. Because of the importance of alignment between assessment forms and learning modalities, this section provides insights to consider when implementing this chapter's assessment-related insights in a range of instructional modalities: entirely remote instruction (in which instruction is completely virtual), hybrid instruction (in which students are physically present in the classroom some days and engage through virtual learning other days), and hyflex instruction (in which some students are physically present in the classroom and other students join at the same time virtually). By sharing these insights, we aim to provide you with suggestions and information that can help you utilize instructional practices that fit well with the instructional modality used in your instruction.

Instructional Modality	Key Suggestions to Consider
Entirely remote	When assessing students who are learning entirely remotely, it's important that we reflect carefully on the remote learning tools that our students have available to them and how each one of those tools can align with the kind of assessment information we want to gather and analyze. For example, if our assessment goal is to collect formative assessment information at the end of a class period or instructional sequence that shows how well students have grasped a key concept, we'll want to select an assessment form that aligns with that objective and with the features of remote learning available to our students. Similarly, if we have the summative assessment goal of determining students' mastery of writing strategies we've taught them, it would be in our best interest to select an assessment method that provides students with opportunities to demonstrate this expertise remotely. While aspects of these remote assessments will certainly vary based on what our students have learned and what remote resources they have available, the most important aspect of assessing using this modality is the alignment between the assessment forms used, the concepts being assessed, and the available resources.
	Since students who participate in hybrid instruction engage in are physically present in the classroom some days and participate in remote learning on others, we recommend aligning assessments with the features of the ways students are engaging on a particular day. When conducting formative assessments, in which you'll use students' insights from a class session or learning activity to gauge their understanding, we suggest making assessment decisions based on how students are learning that day. When students are learning remotely, we recommend selecting ways for them to demonstrate their insights using features of remote learning that are available to them. Similarly, when students are participating in person, they can convey their understandings through exit question responses and class discussions they can share in class.

Instructional Modality	Key Suggestions to Consider
Hybrid	When asking students to complete summative assessments, we suggest aligning the features of the assessment with the ways students will participate on the day the assessment will be submitted. If students will be participating remotely on the day an assessment is due, we recommend giving them assessment options that align with remote learning activities and resources. In contrast, if students will be attending class in person on the day they share summative assessments, we can provide them with assessment options that correspond with that form of engagement. It is also possible to give students options of completing assessments that can be submitted remotely or in person. We teachers can then allow students to submit those assessments remotely or in person based on what best aligns with the assessment they select.
Hyflex	Since hyflex instruction involves all students participating in class at the same time—some in person and others remotely—we recommend selecting formative and summative assessment tools with which students can engage regardless of where they are. For example, students can share formative assessment results and insights through Zoom chat features, Google Docs, or online discussion boards whether they are physically present in the classroom or engaging remotely. This will give you, as the teacher, consistent and useful formative assessment information that you can evaluate regardless of how students are participating. Similarly, students can share their summative assessments using technological tools that all students can access whether they are engaging in person or remotely. For example, if a student chooses to create a website on a social issue and use texts examined in class to inform their understanding of this issue, that student could share the website with their peers whether they are engaging in person or remotely. In addition, a student who writes a piece for an authentic audience could share this work with classmates through Zoom or a similar platform in ways that can be accessed remotely and in person.

Teacher Roles in a New World

A Note About This Chapter and the Others in This Section
This chapter and the two that follow compose Section Three, "Teacher Roles in a New World." The ideas in this section are designed to guide and support teachers as they navigate the unique challenges of the remote learning environment. While the previous chapters in this book address specific instructional tactics and ideas, Chapters Eight, Nine, and Ten focus on big-picture ideas and recommendations that are essential to remote instruction, such as communication and support, reflection, and self-care. As we explore in these chapters, these concepts are important to teaching in general, but are especially significant to remote language arts instruction given the specific challenges and attributes of that instruction.

8

Communicating With and Supporting Students' Caregivers

In this chapter, we examine key strategies that we can use to communicate with and support our students' caregivers as they help students succeed in their remote language arts work. While strong communication and support of students' caregivers is important to effective teaching and learning in general, we feel that it takes on extra significance in remote instruction. Because remote learning has reduced or eliminated the amount of face-to-face contact and the corresponding interaction that were present during in-person school, effective and meaningful communication about what students are learning and the best ways for them to succeed has become increasingly difficult. Due to this challenge, we feel it is important to be as intentional as possible about the ways we communicate with our students' caregivers about curriculum, assignments, students' academic progress, and opportunities for support.

This chapter provides four recommendations that language arts teachers can utilize during remote learning to effectively communicate with our students' caregivers about academic content and learning progress:

◆ Create an online class page that houses important information designed to help students succeed.
◆ Share weekly agendas that describe what students will learn.
◆ Provide caregivers with regular newsletters that communicate important information.
◆ Hold remote conversations with caregivers that illustrate what students learn.

When describing these recommendations, we discuss what each one is and why it is especially important in the context of remote instruction. Now, let's get started on our exploration of ways to maximize the communication with your students and their caregivers during remote learning.

Recommendation One: Create an Online Class Page That Houses Important Information Designed to Help Students Succeed

Our first recommendation for facilitating effective communication with and support of our students' caregivers is to create an online class page or website that is used to house important information that will help facilitate student success. The specific components of this online page can take a variety of forms. For example, based on your school's learning management system, you may have a page in a system such as Google Classroom or Canvas that is specifically dedicated to the material you teach and your students learn. If your school does not have a subscription to such a system, you can make a free website through platforms such as Weebly, Wix, and others. No matter what platform or system you use to construct your website, the most important aspect of the site is that it contains resources and information that will guide students as they complete remote academic work for your language arts course. Since this information is clearly organized for students, it will support caregivers as well: they can visit this site to check on students' assignments and guide them as they work to complete key projects. For example, the site can contain assignment descriptions and rubrics to which students and their caregivers can refer as they work on summative assessments. In addition, you can use the site to store videos you create that explain key concepts, such as a video mini-lesson on important literacy strategies to which students can refer repeatedly. A class website can be an excellent way to house materials that students need, making life easier for them and saving you time: if students and their caregivers need access to important course information, they'll know to look for it on the website (Ruday, 2018). As referenced in multiple instructional snapshots, Taylor's Schoology page is a saving grace and is well used throughout each day. This provides the students a place to instantly look if they miss directions or if they are unable to come to Zoom meetings.

While class websites are outstanding tools for organized and supportive language arts courses in general, they are especially useful for remote teaching and learning. Without the benefit of a structured classroom space that students regularly use, it can be extra difficult to structure the information and resources to which students have access. For example, students working in a face-to-face setting will have regular physical access to materials, tools, and resources that a teacher has set up, and caregivers will know that students will have regular access to this information. Since remote learning often involves students and their caregivers setting up learning environments in alternate spaces, such as the kitchen table, it's especially important that we teachers create well-structured and clearly organized resources students and their caregivers can use to find important course information. Without this access, students and caregivers can become frustrated and anxious, especially given the existing challenges already associated with remote learning. However, with a well-organized and informative website that contains important and easy-to-find course materials, we can help our students succeed and facilitate their caregivers' abilities to support them.

Recommendation Two: Share Weekly Agendas That Describe What Students Will Learn

Along with constructing a website that houses important resources to guide student learning and organization, we recommend sharing with students and their caregivers weekly agendas that discuss what content students will learn that week and what resources they'll need. These agendas, which "are outlines of the material covered for the week and the homework and assignments relevant to each day" (Ruday, 2018, p. 199), provide students with clear information about academic expectations, the work to be done, and the resources they'll need to complete that work. In addition to informing students about important academic work, agendas facilitate caregivers' abilities to support their students: because they provide important information about what students will be doing academically in a particular week and what they'll need to do to complete that work, caregivers can use these agendas to help their student(s) stay on track and to check in with them to ensure that the work is completed. With the information these weekly agendas provide, students will have the information they need to complete academic work, and caregivers will have the details necessary to support them.

Taylor does this by posting a slide each day with the daily schedule. Here the students can see what they need to be doing at each time of the day, and if they are expected in any teacher's Zoom class, those links are right in the slides. The students often keep this up in a separate tab so that they can refer to it throughout the day. All the schedules get posted before the start of the week, allowing the students to review them before diving into the week.

These weekly agendas are especially useful in the context of remote learning, where students do not have the same routines and supports that in-person school provides. By providing students with clear expectations and caregivers with key details about exactly what learning activities are taking place that week, we teachers can provide important details that can facilitate academic success and clear communication during remote learning. We recommend emailing the agendas to students and caregivers at the beginning of each week and posting them on the course website to ensure that everyone involved will have easy access. Making this information readily available remotely will help students be able to access it if they have questions, miss an instructional day, or need to remind themselves of important upcoming work. Caregivers can also access the information when they want to check on what work is assigned for the course and how their student(s) is progressing with that work.

Recommendation Three: Provide Caregivers With Regular Newsletters That Communicate Important Information

In addition to sending students weekly agendas that identify key material to be covered, we recommend creating a course newsletter that you regularly provide to caregivers. These newsletters, which discuss important topics that were recently discussed in the course as well as upcoming assignments and events (Ruday, 2018), are great tools for facilitating strong communication with caregivers. While the weekly agendas described in the previous recommendation provide important information, these newsletters provide additional detail and context that can further develop the sense of communication and support between you as the teacher and students' caregivers. When constructing these newsletters in the past, Sean has divided them into the categories of "What We've Been Up To" and "What's Coming Up," with separate relevant sections related to particular components of literacy instruction, such as reading, writing, and word study (Ruday, 2018). The newsletters can foster a strong sense of communication and let students' caregivers know that you are committed to keeping them informed of key developments in their students' learning. We recommend sending these newsletters to students' caregivers weekly or biweekly via email to further create a sense of regular communication and support.

Taylor does this by sending a message on ClassDojo each week to notify the caregivers of important happenings in the digital classroom. With things changing what seems like every day, it is important to be as transparent as possible with the caregivers. Let them know what *YOU* know, and they will appreciate you. Most caregivers understand the stress of your position and will work with you, but it is necessary that that communication door is open to allow them to ask questions.

We feel that these newsletters are especially important to the context of remote instruction because of the way they facilitate clear and detailed communication between us as teachers and students' caregivers. During remote teaching and learning, it can be more difficult for caregivers to feel connected to their student's teachers and to understand what has been and will be taking place in their student's learning experiences. By sending regular newsletters to our students' caregivers, we teachers clearly convey that we want to build strong relationships with those caregivers during a time when authentic connections can be difficult to create. Regular newsletters are excellent ways to create strong communication with caregivers during any form of instruction but are especially useful for establishing meaningful connections and sharing important information during the challenging time of remote learning.

Recommendation Four: Hold Remote Conversations With Caregivers That Illustrate What Students Learn

This recommendation represents a way for us teachers to show caregivers what their student(s) is or will be learning in their remote English language arts instruction. Katie Van Sluys (2011) describes an example of this in which a school adopted a workshop and process-based approach to writing instruction; since many students' caregivers were unfamiliar with this approach, the school provided them with opportunities to see what this instructional practice looked like in action and shared with them its key components. This approach can be applied to all aspects of language arts instruction: when you are implementing a new instructional practice with which caregivers may be unfamiliar, it's a great idea to invite them to a discussion on that topic. In this discussion, we recommend talking with students' caregivers about the essential features and benefits of the instructional approach you'll implement in your teaching. Doing so can help caregivers understand the instructional methods you'll use and how to support their student(s) if they need extra help. In the context of remote instruction, these conversations can take place virtually to ensure social distance and safety.

We feel that these instructional conversations with caregivers are especially significant during remote learning. Through these conversations, we educators can talk with caregivers about what their language arts instruction will look like in remote contexts. Since remote teaching and learning are new for many so stakeholders in education (such as teachers, students, and caregivers), we can increase caregivers' understanding of what their student(s) will be doing and learning in school through remote conversations about what students will learn and how they'll learn it. For example, if students will be engaging in inquiry-based instruction and analysis, we can hold a remote conversation with caregivers that describes what this instructional practice is, how it will look in remote teaching and learning, what students will do as part of it, and how caregivers can support their students.

Final Thoughts

As the recommendations and ideas discussed in this chapter illustrate, there are a number of important and useful ways for us to communicate with our students and their caregivers during remote learning. These practices are effective ways to facilitate strong communication in any educational context but are especially important in the context of remote teaching and learning, in which communication can be both extra challenging and significant. Communication can be particularly challenging in remote learning because the features of many remote learning formats eliminate the regular routine and structure associated with face-to-face contact and in-person classrooms. Because of these challenges and changes, it is especially important that we are strategic and purposeful when communicating with our students and their caregivers during remote language arts instruction. The information in this chapter will help you communicate with those important individuals in strategic, purposeful, and beneficial ways.

9

Reflecting on Technology

As we've engaged in remote instruction, we have continually reflected on ideas and issues related to the role of technology in our teaching and our students' learning. While technology has played an important role in language arts instruction for years (Richards, 2000; Swenson, Rozema, Young, McGrail, & Whitin, 2005), we feel it has taken on even more significance in the time of increased remote teaching and learning. Since remote instruction has taken on a greater role in education, we believe it is essential for us teachers to reflect on its role in our pedagogical practices. When we reflect on the topic of technology and its role in remote language arts instruction, we find ourselves thinking about the importance of technology use being both strategic and equitable. In this chapter, we explore both of these ideas, focusing on the importance of technology use in remote English language arts instruction that is purposefully selected to align key instructional goals and is equitable for students' technological access, experience levels, and individual needs.

Reflection One: Strategic Technology Use

As educators, we've definitely felt overwhelmed by the many technological tools and resources that we hear and read about. During remote learning, this experience has increased: it seems to us like there is almost always a new instructional technology feature that is being discussed or advertised in teacher-focused environments. While many technological tools and ideas

can be beneficial for effective teaching and learning, we recommend starting your technology-based decision-making process by reflecting on your
instructional goals and students, not specific innovations. As we discuss in
this book's introduction, instead of deciding on a particular technological
resource and designing instruction that fits that program, we suggest first
identifying what you want to teach your students and then selecting the technological tools that you feel will best help your students reach the learning
objectives you've established.

By selecting technological tools strategically, you'll work to ensure that
you're making the choices that best align with the material you're teaching
your students and the students themselves, matching the technology in your
teaching with "students, instruction, and curricular goals" (Young & Bush,
2004, p. 9). If we educators feel that a particular technology resource will have
positive impacts on these three essential components of our pedagogy, we
can be confident that we've made strong decisions related to the uses of technology in our teaching. Conversely, if we're not sure if a technology tool is
a good way to reach our students, facilitate our instruction, and achieve our
curricular goals, then it's in our best interest to further reflect on that resource
and determine if it's the resource we should use. If not, we can consider other
possible tools and decide on one that will best align with all our pedagogical
elements. Without careful reflection on the benefits and uses of available technological resources, we can find ourselves in situations in which technology
is used for the sake of doing instead of because it is the best tool to achieve a
particular learning outcome (Pasternak, 2007).

While the strategic selection of technological tools is important to effective English language arts instruction in general, we feel that this approach
is especially important to remote teaching and learning. Because of the
digital nature of remote instruction, teachers are being asked to consider
a wide range of technological resources and tools, many of which may be
new to them. When we educators examine many new forms of technology,
it's especially important that we keep in mind the features of those tools
and how they optimize the effectiveness of our teaching. As part of this
consideration and reflection, it's important that we think about the many
features of specific technological resources and how those features do or
do not align with specific aspects of our instruction. For example, when
incorporating Zoom into instruction, we can maximize its usefulness to our
teaching and our students' learning if we look at its many aspects and make
strategic decisions about those aspects. Zoom's chat feature, for instance, is
a useful tool in specific aspects of remote instruction, such as when we're
holding a synchronous remote or hybrid class and want students to share
brief responses. On the other hand, if we're looking for a technological tool

that aligns with longer student responses that take more time to compose, we might use Google Docs or online discussion boards. Through the strategic and reflective selection of technological resources, we can maximize our remote English language arts instruction in ways that help our students succeed.

Reflection Two: Equitable Technology Implementation

Like the concept of strategic technology use described in the preceding section, equitable technology access is an essential issue for us educators to carefully consider during remote instruction. In order for us to create effective remote language arts contexts designed to help facilitate student success, we need to reflect on ways to make our instructional technology equitable regarding a number of important issues, such as students' technological access, experience levels, and individual needs. In this section, we look at each of these concepts and explore why they are important to equitable technology implementation in remote language arts instruction.

Students' Technological Access

An essential concept to consider when reflecting on the issue of equity in remote learning is that students have a range of levels of technological access. In a 2020 *Education Week* article titled "Closing COVID-19 Equity Gaps in Schools," author Christine A. Samuels calls for schools to "[c]lose the digital divide to ensure that all students have access to devices, internet, and technology support." As teachers, it is important that we are aware that our students may have different levels of access related to these topics. We can use this awareness to inform our communication with students and their caregivers as well as our instruction. For example, we can remind students and caregivers of any technological and accessibility supports that the school provides students and families, such as those that Samuels describes. In addition, we can build variation and flexibility into our instruction that account for different levels of students' technological access. One such way is by providing students who may not be able to join synchronous classes due to technological access issues with alternate ways to learn information and convey their knowledge. For example, students could complete asynchronous assignments that may involve reading articles, reflecting on them, and watching short, prerecorded videos if their technology allows. These students could then share their ideas and responses via technological tools that require less bandwidth, such as emails, online discussion boards, or Google Docs. Of course, this is just one potential example: the specific tactics you'll use to support your students will depend on their individual situations and the assignments you give them. While certain aspects of these features will vary across contexts, we strongly encourage you to keep in mind that students may have different levels of access to technology and to factor this issue into your instructional decision-making.

Students' Technological Experience Levels

In addition to reflecting on students' technological access and making appropriate accommodations in our instruction and communication with students, it is also important that we recognize that our students may have different levels of experience with technological tools and programs. This variation in experience is another form of the "digital divide" that Christine Samuels (2020) refers to in the previously mentioned article, "Closing COVID-19 Equity Gaps in Schools." Our awareness of the potential variation in students' experience will help us facilitate equitable instruction based on understandings of this concept. We can incorporate this awareness into our instruction in multiple ways. At the beginning of the school year, we can ask students to complete surveys seen only by us in which they assess their comfort with various technological tools and innovations. We can then use these survey results to support our students and even decide which tools we want to use in our instruction. When we implement technological tools and resources in our teaching, it's important that we take some time to familiarize students with those innovations and how to use them and to answer questions they have. By doing this, we can ensure students' common understanding about technological tools and avoid assumptions about students' experience and familiarity levels. While students work, we can then check in with them individually about their comfort with technological tools and provide them with the support that will help them use those resources.

Students' Individual Needs

In order to reflect on equitable and student-centered technology use in remote English language arts instruction, we also need to consider students' individual needs and how we can use technological tools and resources to meet those needs. Since the specific learning needs of your students will be unique to them, we encourage you to communicate with those students, their caregivers, school administrators, and others involved to identify the best ways to meet their needs during remote instruction. The website Educating All Learners (2020)—www.educatingalllearners.org—provides a number of resources related to making remote teaching and learning as accessible as possible to all students, including those with disabilities, explaining that "[a]s schools shift to online learning, the needs of students with disabilities are too often put on the back burner—instead, they must be considered from the beginning" (para. 2). Some practices that we recommend incorporating to help all students learn are using captioning on videos to help all students access the material, holding one-on-one conferences with students as they work on remote assessments to provide them with individualized support, and being flexible with the amount of processing and work time students are able to take on projects. These are some overarching suggestions that can help remote instruction align with students' needs. The additional and more specific steps you take in your instruction will be based on your students and the best ways to support them as individual learners.

Final Thoughts

The technology-related issues discussed in this chapter have long been part of the conversation about effective teaching but have taken on special significance during the time of increased remote instruction. We encourage you to think carefully and reflectively about the technological choices you make during your remote language arts instruction. This thoughtful reflection will help you build an equitable learning experience for your students. When we align our technology use with key learning goals and think carefully about issues of equity in our technology implementation, we work to create meaningful and inclusive remote instruction. There are so many forms of remote technology use and implementation options available to us teachers in today's educational context. The reflective ideas described in this chapter will help you incorporate them in ways that facilitate student learning, access, and equity.

10

Taking Care of Yourself

The stress (Gallup, 2014) and potential burnout (Richards, 2012) of teachers have long been an issue in education. Now, in the current context of remote teaching and learning in the COVID-19 era, this issue has become even more significant: teachers are experiencing "immense challenges, and exhaustion" (Singer, 2020, para. 6) brought on by the intense demands of teaching remotely in a pandemic-altered world. Since the already-significant challenge of taking care of oneself as a teacher has grown in difficulty with increased remote instruction and the associated stressors of COVID-19, we believe that it's especially important that teachers are intentional about focusing on self-care during this time. In this chapter, we share five recommendations regarding ways to create work–life balance, take care of yourself, and manage the stresses associated with remote teaching:

1. Don't wait to engage in self-care activities.
2. Schedule times to disconnect.
3. Create time to share and vent about your experiences.
4. Create times to socialize about anything but teaching.
5. Get lost in a passion.

By implementing these recommendations in ways that align with your interests and preferred self-care activities, you take important steps to ensure that you take care of yourself, which will ultimately maximize your productivity, enjoyment, and longevity as a teacher (Ruday, 2018). Now, let's reflect on these suggestions, why they're useful, and how they can enhance your work as a remote language arts teacher.

Recommendation One: Don't Wait to Engage in Self-Care Activities

Sometimes, we teachers might think of self-care activities as things to help us decompress and re-center when we get stressed and overwhelmed. While this can certainly be true, we also encourage you to think of self-care activities as things to do on a regular basis before you experience those feelings. This approach makes our participation in self-care activities proactive instead of reactive and can increase the likelihood that we'll participate in those activities. For example, if someone's go-to self-care tactic is yoga, it would not be in their best interest to wait until they get stressed to do yoga. By doing it regularly, before feeling anxious or overwhelmed, they can ensure that they engage in their self-care activities, which can then ultimately help them deal better with stressors they might encounter. These practices establish a proactive routine that will help us continuously engage in self-care and regularly achieve all the benefits that self-care practices provide. Of course, it's also a good idea to take additional self-care measures when feeling stressed. The recommendation we focus on here is to make sure to participate in some self-care activities before stress sets in to proactively take care of yourself and help you get in a regular routine of doing so.

Recommendation Two: Schedule Times to Disconnect

Another proactive self-care tactic we recommend is scheduling times to disconnect from all teaching-related communication, such as email, notifications from learning management systems, and other similar messages. While scheduling times to disconnect from work is important in general, we feel that this is especially important in the context of remote instruction. Because of the digital nature of remote instruction, it's so easy to feel like we educators are always at work. We may receive emails and notifications at all hours of the day, and it's possible to feel called to respond to those messages as soon as we get them. Because of this, we feel that it's essential to delineate times in which you are disconnected from all work-related communication. You might want to use this time to enjoy a self-care activity or just use it for anything at all. For example, Sean will disconnect and work out, read a book, play the Xbox with his 13-year-old, or participate in another activity altogether. No matter what you choose to do during this time, the most important aspect of this recommendation is to be as proactive and regular as possible about scheduling times to disconnect from teaching-related communication to take care of yourself and give yourself a break from the continued pressures and expectations of remote learning.

Recommendation Three: Create Time to Share and Vent About Your Experiences

While it's important to unplug and take time away from the pressures and stresses of remote language arts instruction, we also recommend creating time to share and vent about your experiences, challenges, frustrations, and successes. Depending on your preferences, you might want to do this with fellow teachers or with others who are not involved in teaching. Whether or not the individuals with whom you share are educators, it's important to find a group of people with whom you feel safe, comfortable, and able to share key aspects of the remote instruction experience. Since so many components of remote teaching are new and challenging, we recommend taking the time to discuss and process your experiences with others. Doing so will create opportunities to express the challenges you're experiencing and can create a sense of community that can help all involved feel supported in a challenging time. You may even want to develop multiple communities by reaching out to teachers at other schools, former colleagues and classmates, friends, and relatives. In today's world, we can use features like Zoom, FaceTime, and the like to communicate with others and benefit from the opportunities for the interaction they provide.

Recommendation Four: Create Times to Socialize About Anything But Teaching

This recommendation works with the ideas in Recommendation Three to emphasize the importance of purposeful communication to self-care. While we believe, as discussed in Recommendation Three, that it's important to take time to vent and talk about the challenges associated with remote teaching, we also feel that it's important that educators create times to socialize about anything but teaching. Although we're extremely passionate about teaching and love discussing issues and topics related to education, we believe that socializing about other topics goes a long way toward avoiding burnout.

Since so many teachers are experiencing symptoms of burnout during remote learning in the time of COVID-19 (Singer, 2020), we recommend engaging in social activities that will create opportunities for you to talk about other interests and take your mind off of education-related stresses. These conversations about non-work-related topics can provide balance and rest in a stressful time when both of those entities can be difficult to find.

Recommendation Five: Get Lost in a Passion

To take care of ourselves amid the challenges and pressures of remote instruction, we recommend immersing yourself in something that you're passionate about and enjoy. By engaging in something you love doing, you can bring yourself joy and excitement, which can help you feel rejuvenated and able to take on challenging tasks. While these specific passions will take on different forms for many of us, the key component they'll all have in common is the way they allow the individual who is interested in that topic to focus on and derive enjoyment from that activity. So whether you love watching baking shows, listening to a particular musical artist, reading page-turning works by a favorite author, knitting, playing a video game with friends, or anything else, we encourage you to devote some time to engaging in that passion. The feeling of joy and escape that these activities can help you feel happy and rested, which can then help you approach difficult situations as effectively as possible.

Final Thoughts

In order to be effective teachers during remote instruction, it's essential that we take care of ourselves. While it can be easy to forget to prioritize self-care, we strongly recommend making it a point to take care of yourself. The ideas discussed in this chapter about proactively and purposefully engaging in self-care can help us educators guard against feeling overwhelmed, exhausted, and stressed while teaching remotely. When putting these ideas into action in your own life, we encourage you to take time and reflect on the activities that can give you joy and help you feel energized. Once you've identified those activities, we recommend leaning into them as key self-care practices. We strongly believe that self-care makes us as educators more effective for our students: by taking care of ourselves, we'll have the energy, patience, and clarity to be as effective as possible for our students. In other words, it will help us educators be the great teachers that we are capable of being.

IV

Resources

11

Key Takeaway Ideas

Now that you've read the first ten chapters of this book, you've developed a wide range of ideas and practices to use when optimizing the effectiveness of remote language arts instruction. The insights and approaches we've shared are designed to help you and your students engage in meaningful remote instruction that engages students, centers their positionalities, values equity, helps them learn important content, and aligns with the features of remote teaching and learning. With these core ideas in mind, we present in this chapter five key takeaway ideas to reflect on as you put the insights and examples described in this book into action in your instruction:

- ◆ Reflect on and purposefully select technological tools.
- ◆ Prioritize community building in remote instruction.
- ◆ Emphasize collaboration and interaction.
- ◆ Center students' ideas and experiences.
- ◆ Be purposeful about communication and self-care.

These recommendations are designed to synthesize important ideas in this book and provide key concluding ideas to keep in mind during your remote language arts instruction. As you examine them, we recommend thinking about how you'll implement each of these suggestions into your teaching, drawing on the ideas and examples shared in this book. Now, let's jump into these recommendations and consider each of them in detail.

Recommendation One: Reflect On and Purposefully Select Technological Tools

One of the most important aspects of effective remote language arts instruction is reflecting on and purposefully selecting technological tools. As we've discussed in this book, there are so many apps, programs, and innovations available to teachers engaging in remote teaching and learning that it's easy to feel overwhelmed by the seemingly countless options. These many possibilities not only can result in teachers feeling anxious about which ones to pick but also can make it difficult to select the technological tools that best align with student learning. To address this issue, we strongly recommend reflecting on which resources best align with learning goals and student needs and then selecting tools that correspond with those concepts.

These learning goals and student needs can take a range of forms, such as the instructional objectives you want your students to understand, the ways you want them to demonstrate their knowledge, and how the instructional activities you want them to use align with the modality in which students are working. For example, if your instructional goal is for students to think about and respond to key issues in a text they've read, we recommend thinking about the remote learning tools that you feel best align with this practice and how those tools work in the modality you and your students are using. Google Docs, for instance, can be effective ways for students who are sharing ideas in a synchronous remote class to reflect on and express detailed insights about a topic because students can see their peers' responses come through in real time and respond immediately. In contrast, if students are doing this activity in a remote asynchronous modality, online discussion boards can work well—this technological resource facilitates thoughtful responses that students can share with one another and respond to over time. The technological resources you use will certainly vary based on specific contextual elements; we encourage you to carefully and thoughtfully reflect on the tools you use to ensure that they best align with important learning goals and student needs.

Recommendation Two: Prioritize Community Building in Remote Instruction

We strongly recommend making community building a point of emphasis in your remote language arts instruction. While creating a learning community certainly takes on a different form in remote teaching and learning than it does in a traditional in-person classroom, it is still an essential aspect of students' academic and personal successes for a variety of reasons. The relationships we build with our students can make a significant impact on the quality of their experiences in school and maximize their academic performance (Quin, 2016). When we construct strong and supportive learning environments for our students, we can help them feel safe, collaborate with others, and take risks (Aspen Institute, 2017). These benefits of community building are even more important when we consider that students report that they've experienced less motivation and academic success in remote learning (Nierenberg, 2020). By building a strong community of learners in our remote instruction, we can help our students succeed academically through supportive communities that facilitate their abilities to take risks and feel safe.

To intentionally and purposefully construct a learning community that maximizes students' feelings of support and academic success, we recommend reflecting on the essential aspects that you feel should be present in a strong learning community and then thinking about how those components would look in a remote context. For example, if one component that you greatly value in a learning community is the opportunity for students to get to know each other by sharing their opinions about topics that matter to them, you can ask students fun, get-to-know-you questions in the Zoom chat box, on Google Classroom, or through another technological resource before or after class. If something that you believe makes a strong learning community is the opportunity for students to incorporate their own interests into assignments, you can construct remote learning projects in which students have choice and opportunities to express their interests. In addition, if you value a community in which the teacher expresses their authentic personality with the class, you can build in opportunities during mini-lessons and class discussions to share your interests and help your students get to know you as a person. When we build strong remote learning communities, we are seeking to create a supportive learning environment in which students feel safe; while such a community will look different than an in-person one, the core idea of supporting our students remains consistent.

Recommendation Three: Emphasize Collaboration and Interaction

This recommendation builds off of the ideas discussed in Recommendation Two: as you build a strong and supportive learning community with your students, we suggest purposefully emphasizing collaboration and interaction in your remote language arts instruction. Opportunities for students to engage in meaningful collaboration and learning-related conversations are important to effective learning in general (Hurst et al., 2013) and are especially significant to remote learning (Kyei-Blankson et al., 2019), in which students don't have the same natural opportunities for interaction and discussion with classmates and teachers that exist in traditional face-to-face learning. By providing our students with collaborative and interactive experiences, we can help them experience the benefits of being in a supportive and motivational learning community that contains meaningful opportunities for interaction.

The collaborative and interactive work in which students participate can take a range of forms; we recommend purposefully varying the structures of these activities based on the goals of the activities. For example, some collaborative work that students complete together is well suited to the features of Google Docs or Google Slides, others might be best aligned with a breakout room, and others might work best with responses written in a chat box. We believe that all these collaboration tools can provide beneficial experiences for students and do not feel that any specific tool is better than others; rather, we feel that the best collaboration resource to use is the one that best aligns with a particular assignment, your students, and the instructional modality you and your students use. No matter the specific form your students' collaboration takes, we recommend talking with students about how to use the collaboration and why that tool will help them collaborate in ways that align with the assignment. By sharing this information, you'll ensure that your students have clear expectations for the activity, and you'll build a transparent and purposeful instructional environment that will help students understand the benefits that will come from the activities in which they're engaging.

Recommendation Four: Center Students' Ideas and Experiences

An important component of building a student-centered, motivational, and equitable remote learning environment is centering students' ideas and experiences in our instructional practices. To do this, we recommend focusing on the key principles of culturally relevant (Ladson-Billings, 1995) and culturally sustaining pedagogy (Paris, 2012) described in Chapter Five of this book, as well as the inquiry-based approach discussed in Chapter Six. These pedagogical approaches place students' authentic experiences in central roles in the language arts curriculum. Culturally relevant and sustaining pedagogy facilitates authentic connections between concepts that students learn in school and their out-of-school lives, creating space for students by recognizing and valuing their realities, perspectives, and identities (Lyiscott, 2019) and incorporating the literacies that are authentic to their lived experiences

(Duncan-Andrade & Morrell, 2005). Similarly, inquiry-based language arts instruction's focus on big-picture, thought-provoking essential questions (McTighe & Wiggins, 2013) creates natural opportunities to craft student-centered learning experiences, especially since these questions can be easily and closely aligned with students' curiosities and interests (Ruday & Caprino, 2021).

Fortunately, the structure of remote teaching and learning can create opportunities for students to learn in their own communities and investigate topics that matter to them individually. In remote instruction, students spend more time learning in their homes and communities than they would in a traditional face-to-face context; we teachers can use this feature to construct additional ways for students to bring their communities, cultures, and interests into their learning. For instance, if students are engaging in an activity in which they look for examples of a writing strategy in their out-of-school lives, we can encourage them to look at the many forms of text that exist around them in organic and authentic ways in their communities. This community-based application can work toward culturally relevant and sustaining pedagogy and create a learning environment for students in which the concept of "text" has authentic applications that go beyond what is present in school. Similarly, when students investigate inquiries that are centered on essential questions related to issues in their lives and communities, they can draw on texts from and related to topics that matter to them. Students can then remotely share these ideas, connections, and responses through tools and features of remote learning.

Recommendation Five: Be Purposeful About Communication and Self-Care

To maximize your productivity, effectiveness, and health during the stresses and challenges of remote teaching and learning, we recommend being purposeful and proactive regarding the important topics of communication and self-care. By taking intentional and thoughtful measures in relation to these concepts, we educators can build strong and supportive relationships with our students and their caregivers while also ensuring that we take care of ourselves. While there are certainly differences between communicating effectively with others and engaging in self-care, we feel that there are also important similarities between these actions: they both require purposeful action, and they both contribute to our overall well-being and effectiveness, thereby helping us teach well in a difficult time.

When we communicate effectively with our students and their caregivers, we can create smooth and positive learning experiences for all involved. If we provide them with clear information and organized structures in which that information is conveyed, they'll know where to go to find important course details and will be able to use the structures you've created to answer questions on their own. If students and caregivers can do this efficiently and independently, you'll be able to spend more time on your instruction and less time answering questions. In other words, proactive and purposeful communication can increase our efficiency and effectiveness. Similarly, this approach can be applied to self-care strategies: by taking care of ourselves using the tactics and recommendations described in Chapter Ten, we can ensure that we're prioritizing our mental and physical health before we feel overwhelmed and stressed. We encourage you to create communication and self-care plans so that you can proactively address the challenges and maximize your effectiveness and health.

Final Thoughts

We wrote this book with two primary goals in mind: (1) to help teachers think about the best ways to teach language arts and (2) to provide recommendations, ideas, and examples to help teachers put these ideas into action in their remote instruction. The information you've examined in this book will help you achieve these two goals; the range of topics we describe in this text and the variety of recommendations we share are designed to provide a comprehensive perspective on how to maximize the effectiveness of your remote language arts instruction. By putting these ideas into action, you'll make purposeful instructional choices that center your students and are informed by strategic selections of remote learning tools that align with key learning goals, your individual students, and the instructional modalities in which you and your students are working. We know that remote teaching is not easy, but the information we share in this book about effective language arts instruction, what it can look like in remote contexts, and how to implement it in your own practice will guide you as you support your students. Now that you've completed this book, we hope that you're able to say, "I know about high-quality language arts instruction, and I know how to implement it in remote learning!"

References

Aspen Institute. (2017). *Putting it all together*. The Aspen Institute's National Commission on Social, Emotional, and Academic Development. Retrieved from www.aspeninstitute.org/publications/putting-it-all-together/

Bishop, R. S. (1990). Mirrors, windows, and sliding glass doors. *Perspectives: Choosing and Using Books for the Classroom*, 6(3), ix–xi.

Dolghan, J., Kelly, K., & Zelkha, S. (2010). *Authentic assessments for the English classroom*. Urbana, IL: National Council of Teachers of English.

Duncan-Andrade, J., & Morrell, E. (2005). Turn up that radio, teacher: Popular cultural pedagogy in new century urban schools. *Journal of School Leadership*, 15(3), 284–304.

Educating all Learners. (2020). Retrieved from https://educatingalllearners.org/

Fletcher, R., & Portalupi, J. (2001). *Writing workshop: The essential guide*. Portsmouth, NH: Heinemann.

Gallup, Inc. (2014). *State of America's schools report*. Retrieved from www.gallup.com/education/269648/state-america-schools-report.aspx

Gay, G. (2002). *Culturally responsive teaching: Theory, research and practice*. New York, NY: Teacher's College Press.

Grisham, D. L., & Wolsey, T. D. (2006). Recentering the middle school classroom as a vibrant learning community: Students, literacy, and technology intersect. *Journal of Adolescent & Adult Literacy*, 49(8), 648–660.

Harvey, S., & Goudvis, A. (2017). *Strategies that work, third edition: Teaching comprehension for engagement, understanding, and building knowledge, grades K-8*. Portsmouth, NH: Stenhouse.

Hurst, B., Wallace, R., & Nixon, S. B. (2013). The impact of social interaction on student learning. *Reading Horizons: A Journal of Literacy and Language Arts*, 52(4), 375–398.

International Literacy Association. (2017). *Literacy assessment: What everyone needs to know*. Retrieved from www.literacyworldwide.org/docs/default-source/where-we-stand/literacy-assessment-brief.pdf?sfvrsn=efd4a68e_4

Jones, L. M., & Mitchell, K. J. (2016). Defining and measuring youth digital citizenship. *New Media & Society*, 18(9), 2063–2079.

Juliani, A. J. (2015). *Inquiry and innovation in the classroom: Using 20% time, genius hour, and PBL to drive student success*. New York, NY: Routledge.

Krebs, D., & Zvi, G. (2015). *The genius hour guidebook: Fostering passion, wonder, and inquiry in the classroom.* New York, NY: Routledge.

Kyei-Blankson, L., Ntuli, E., & Donnelly, H. (2019). Establishing the importance of interaction and presence to student learning in online environments. *Journal of Interactive Learning Research, 30*(4), 539–560.

Ladson-Billings, G. (1995). But that's just good teaching! The case for culturally relevant pedagogy. *Theory into Practice, 34*(3), 159–165.

Lyiscott, J. (2019). *Black appetite. White food.* New York, NY: Routledge Eye on Education.

Machado, E. (2017). Culturally sustaining pedagogy in the literacy classroom. *Literacy now.* Retrieved from www.literacyworldwide.org/blog/literacy-now/2017/05/31/culturally-sustaining-pedagogy-in-the-literacy-classroom

McTighe, J., & Wiggins, G. (2013). *Essential questions: Opening doors to student understanding.* Alexandria, VA: ASCD.

Myroup, S. (2020). Writing conferences for effective instruction. *Virginia English Journal, 70*(1). https://digitalcommons.bridgewater.edu/vej/vol70/iss1/8/#

National Council of Teachers of English. (2016). *Professional knowledge for the teaching of writing.* Retrieved from https://ncte.org/statement/teaching-writing/

National Council of Teachers of English. (2018). *Literacy assessment: Definitions, principles, and practices.* Retrieved from https://ncte.org/statement/assessmentframingst/

National Council of Teachers of English. (2019). *The act of reading: Instructional foundations and policy guidelines.* Retrieved from https://ncte.org/statement/the-act-of-reading/

National Council of Teachers of English. (2020). *Expanding formative assessment for equity and agency.* Retrieved from https://ncte.org/statement/expanding-formative-assessment/

National Council of Teachers of English & International Reading Association. (1996). *NCTE/IRA standards for the English language arts.* Retrieved from https://ncte.org/resources/standards/ncte-ira-standards-for-the-english-language-arts/

National Writing Project & Nagin, C. (2006). *Because writing matters: Improving student writing in our schools.* San Francisco, CA: Jossey-Bass.

Nierenberg, A. (2020). Students, parents and teachers tell their stories of remote learning. *The New York Times.* Retrieved from www.nytimes.com/2020/10/14/education/learning/students-parents-teachers-remote-stories.html

Palacio, R. J. (2012). *Wonder.* New York, NY: Alfred A. Knopf.

Paris, D. (2012). Culturally sustaining pedagogy: A needed change in stance, terminology, and practice. *Educational Researcher, 41*(3), 93–97.

Pasternak, D. L. (2007). Is technology used as practice? A survey analysis of preservice English teachers' perceptions and classroom practices. *Contemporary Issues in Technology and Teacher Education, 7*(3), 140–157. Retrieved from https://citejournal.org/vol7/iss3/languagearts/article1.cfm.

Quin, D. (2016). Longitudinal and contextual associations between teacher–student relationships and student engagement: A systematic review. *Review of Educational Research, 87*(2), 345–387.

Responsive Classroom. (2016, June 7). *What is morning meeting?* Retrieved from www.responsiveclassroom.org/what-is-morning-meeting/

Rhine, S. & Bailey, M. (2011). Collaborative software and focused distraction in the classroom. *The Journal of Technology and Teacher Education, 19*(4), 423–447.

Richards, G. (2000). Why use computer technology? *English Journal, 90*(2), 38–41.

Richards, J. (2012). Teacher stress and coping strategies: A national snapshot. *Educational Forum, 76*, 299–316.

Robb, L. (2003). *Teaching reading in social studies, science, and math.* New York, NY: Scholastic.

Rosenblatt, L. M. (1968). *Literature as exploration.* New York, NY: Noble and Nobel.

Rosenblatt, L. M. (1978). *The reader, the text, the poem: The transactional theory of the literary work.* Carbondale, IL: Southern Illinois University Press.

Ruday, S. (2016). *The multimedia writing toolkit: Helping students incorporate graphics and videos for authentic purposes, grades 3–8.* New York, NY: Routledge.

Ruday, S. (2018). *The first-year English teacher's guidebook: Strategies for success.* New York, NY: Routledge.

Ruday, S., & Caprino, K. (2021). *Inquiry-based literature instruction in the 6–12 classroom: A hands-on guide for deeper learning.* New York, NY: Routledge.

Samuels, C. A. (2020). Closing COVID-19 equity gaps in schools. *Education Week.* Retrieved from www.edweek.org/leadership/closing-covid-19-equity-gaps-in-schools/2020/09

Singer, N. (2020). Teaching in the pandemic: "This is not sustainable." *The New York Times.* Retrieved from www.nytimes.com/2020/11/30/us/teachers-remote-learning-burnout.html

Swenson, J., Rozema, R., Young, C. A., McGrail, E., & Whitin, P. (2005). Beliefs about technology and the preparation of English teachers: Beginning the conversation. *Contemporary Issues in Technology and Teacher Education, 5*(3/4), 210–236.

Van Sluys, K. (2011). *Becoming writers in the elementary classroom.* Urbana, IL: NCTE.

Wiggins, G. (1998). *Education assessment: Designing assessments to inform and improve student performance.* San Francisco, CA: Jossey-Bass.

Wiggins, G., & McTighe, J. (2005). *Understanding by design.* Upper Saddle River, NJ: Pearson.

Young, C. A., & Bush, J. (2004). Teaching the English language arts with technology: A critical approach and pedagogical framework. *Contemporary Issues in Technology and Teacher Education, 4*(1), 1–22.

V

Appendices

Appendix A
Forms, Templates, and Graphic Organizers

This appendix contains resources designed to help you put the ideas discussed in this book into action in your own remote language arts instruction. The forms, templates, and graphic organizers provided here will guide your instructional practice and help you engage your students in effective remote language arts learning.

Text You Used	Example of the Focal Strategy or Concept in the Text	Why You Feel the Strategy or Concept is Important to the Effectiveness of the Text

Figure 3.1 Graphic Organizer for Published Text Analysis

Student's name:

Date:

The day's focal strategy:

Title and Brief Description of the Student's Piece	A Specific Strength of the Piece You Identified	A Concrete Suggestion for Improvement You Shared With the Student

Figure 3.2 Writing Conference Graphic Organizer

A Key Aspect of Background Knowledge You'll Focus on Building in Your Mini-Lesson	Key Vocabulary You'll Pre-teach in Your Mini Lesson	Key Reading Strategies You'll Address in Your Mini-Lesson

Figure 4.1 Mini-Lesson Identification Chart

The Text You're Teaching	A Key Issue in the Text	Why Understanding This Issue Will Benefit Students	Some Activities You'll Use to Help Students Engage With This Issue

Figure 4.2 Key Issues Planning Chart

Writing	Reading	Language Study
• Strong verbs • Specific nouns • Connotation-rich words • Engaging leads • Sensory detail	• Inferences • Connections • Analysis of mood • Predictions • Context clues	• Domain-specific vocabulary relevant to students' authentic experiences • Examples of word roots students encounter in their out-of-school lives

Figure 5.1 Examples of Literacy Concepts and Strategies

Assessment	Brief Description	Why It Aligns With Remote Teaching and Learning
Website on social issue	Students can create websites on social issues reflected in texts they've read, using those texts as support.	This assessment format provides students with authentic opportunities for students to share their ideas in ways that are meant to be created remotely for remote audiences, creating a strong alignment with remote instruction.
Podcast on social issue	Similar to the previously described websites, students can create podcasts on social issues in the texts they've read and use those texts to support their ideas.	Podcasts can make outstanding remote assessments because they are meant to be shared remotely and align with both individual and collaborative work. For example, students can create podcasts on their own, or they can interview others and remotely incorporate their perspectives.
Writing for real-world audiences	Students can write on issues that matter to them and share those perspectives in authentic ways, such as posting them on Google Docs and sharing those links on social media, writing letters to online newspapers and magazines, and writing blog posts and comments that are read by authentic audiences.	By writing for real-world audiences, students can see that writing is not something just done for school: it can be done to share ideas in authentic, real-world ways. Through doing this, students are able to gain practice and experience with writing concepts while also sharing their perspectives with others who go beyond their teacher and classmates.

Assessment	Brief Description	Why It Aligns With Remote Teaching and Learning
Virtual panel conferences and webinars	In virtual panel conferences and webinars, students share ideas about key concepts they've studied and their unique perspectives on these ideas. Students present on concepts that are thematically aligned but offer their unique perspectives on these issues.	These panels and webinars provide excellent opportunities for remote learning evaluation because they create ways for students to express ideas and apply key understandings. This assessment format aligns well with culturally relevant and inquiry-based instruction because it provides excellent opportunities for students to provide their unique perspectives on conceptually aligned topics.
Infographics and one-pagers	Infographics and one-pagers are documents that use graphics and images to express key ideas about a character, text, theme, or concept. They allow students to combine words and images to effectively convey their ideas.	These documents, through their combination of visual features and student-created texts, purposefully incorporate digital tools in ways that call for students to express their knowledge. They are created and shared online in ways that align with features of remote learning and provide teachers with clear understandings of how well students have grasped key content.

Figure 7.1 Possible Authentic Summative Assessments

Appendix B
A Guide for Book Studies

This book is well suited for groups of teachers using the text as a book study as they meet and discuss the successes and challenges they're experiencing in their language arts instruction. If you're interested in discussing the ideas, information, and suggestions in this text with other teachers in order to learn with and from them, we recommend using this guide to facilitate your conversations. The guide provides key discussion questions to consider as you read and reflect on each of the book's chapters. These questions are designed to help you think about key issues in the text and to spark conversations with your colleagues about how you can apply the book's information to your own remote language arts instruction.

Discussion Questions—Introduction

- ◆ Early in this introductory chapter, we list a number of questions that we (Sean and Taylor) have asked ourselves about remote language arts instruction. Select one of those questions that stands out to you as important and relevant. Why does this question resonate with you?
- ◆ This chapter discusses the information and topics we explore in this book. What is a topic you're especially interested to explore?

Discussion Questions—Chapter One: Building a Learning Community and Supporting Student Behavior in Remote Instruction

- ◆ What are some ways you have built strong learning communities in your face-to-face classes? Reflect on some key features of those communities. While the methods of engagement will certainly be different, what are some ways you believe you could build similarly strong communities that help students feel included and support strong behavior in your remote instruction?
- ◆ In this chapter, we provide five recommendations:
  - Conduct informal check-ins about noncurricular topics.
  - Share your own excitement, vulnerability, and personality.
  - Model what curiosity and learning look like for you.
  - Center students' identities and experiences in the curriculum.
  - Create class agreements that prioritize a supportive environment.

What is a way you have done or will do one of these things in your remote instruction?

Discussion Questions—Chapter Two: Class Discussion and Student Collaboration in a New Era

- ◆ Based on the ideas and information in this chapter, what are some methods and tools you'll use to engage your students in remote class discussion and in collaborative activities?
- ◆ In this chapter's recommendations section, we describe a variety of suggestions for maximizing the effectiveness of class discussions. What are some practices you'll incorporate to make your students' class discussions and collaborations as effective as possible?

Discussion Questions—Chapter Three: A New Format of Writing and Grammar Instruction

- ◆ Based on your reading of this chapter and your experiences, what do you believe are some especially important aspects of effective writing and grammar instruction?

◆ In this chapter, we explain that "[w]hile the specific methods of delivery and collaboration will certainly differ, we feel that all these components of effective writing instruction can be achieved in remote learning." With this in mind, which remote learning tools and features will you use as you support your students' understanding of writing strategies and grammatical concepts?

Discussion Questions—Chapter Four: Reading Instruction in the Remote Environment

◆ In this chapter, we discuss reading instruction that focuses on what students do before, during, and after learning (Robb, 2003) and ways to connect these stages of reading instruction to remote learning. Now that you've explored these concepts and the information discussed in this chapter, reflect on how you would guide students through this instructional process during remote learning, focusing on ways you would create meaningful experiences for students before they read a text, while they read it, and after they read the text. Some questions that can help you reflect on this topic include the following:
  – What are some specific practices and tools you would implement? Why do you think those practices and tools will benefit your students?
  – What are some remote learning resources you would use to support your students as they engage remotely with works they read? Why do you feel these resources would be effective ways to support students?

Discussion Questions—Chapter Five: Culturally Relevant and Sustaining Teaching and Learning in Remote Contexts

◆ In this chapter, we explain that "[a]s Ladson-Billings (1995) and Paris (2012) describe, culturally relevant and culturally sustaining pedagogy is essential to creating equitable learning experiences for students" and "is characterized by instructional practices that value and center students' identities, which helps create opportunities for students' academic success." How have you centered students' identities in your language arts instruction? How do you feel doing so contributed to equitable learning experiences for your students?

◆ What are some ways you will use the tools and features of remote learning as you incorporate culturally relevant and sustaining pedagogy in your instruction?

Discussion Questions—Chapter Six: The Role of Inquiry in Remote Teaching and Learning

◆ Reflect on the features of essential questions (McTighe & Wiggins, 2013) and the attributes of inquiry-based language arts instruction (Ruday & Caprino, 2021) discussed in this chapter. Based on this information and the other ideas discussed in the chapter, why do you think inquiry-based language arts instruction can create strong learning experiences for students?

◆ How will you use the attributes of remote instruction to create inquiry-based experiences for your students?

Discussion Questions—Chapter Seven: Assessing Student Learning

◆ In this chapter, we discuss the importance of purposeful formative and summative assessments in language arts instruction. What are some formative and summative assessments that have worked well for you in your instruction? What do you think made them effective?

◆ We also describe in this chapter a range of tactics teachers can incorporate when remotely implementing formative and summative assessments. What are some ways you will remotely assess student learning in your instruction?

Discussion Questions—Chapter Eight: Communicating With and Supporting Students' Caregivers

◆ What are some ways that communication with and support of students' caregivers has changed for you during remote instruction?

◆ In this chapter, we provide four recommendations for communicating with and supporting students' caregivers:

- Create an online class page that houses important information designed to help students succeed.
- Share weekly agendas that describe what students will learn.
- Provide caregivers with regular newsletters that communicate important information.
- Hold remote conversations with caregivers that illustrate what students learn.

Select one of these recommendations that especially stands out to you and reflect on how you'll put it into practice in your instruction.

Discussion Questions—Chapter Nine: Reflecting on Technology

◆ One of the key concepts discussed in this chapter is the strategic use of technology. As we explain in the chapter, "[w]hile many technological tools and ideas can be beneficial for effective teaching and learning, we recommend starting your technology-based decision-making process by reflecting on your instructional goals and students, not specific innovations." What are some ways you can apply the concept of strategic technology use to your remote language arts instruction?

◆ In this chapter, we also discuss the importance of equity-related issues in instructional technology, explaining that "[i]n order for us to create effective remote language arts contexts designed to help facilitate student success, we need to reflect on ways to make our instructional technology equitable regarding a number of important issues, such as students' technological access, experience levels, and individual needs." What are some ways you will promote equity in your instructional technology use?

Discussion Questions—Chapter Ten: Taking Care of Yourself

◆ What are some self-care activities that help you feel energized and centered in stressful times?

◆ In this chapter, we provide five recommendations for taking care of yourself during the stresses of remote instruction:
- Don't wait to engage in self-care activities.
- Schedule times to disconnect.

- Create time to share and vent about your experiences.
- Create times to socialize about anything but teaching.
- Get lost in a passion.

Select one of these recommendations and reflect on how you might put it into action.

Discussion Questions—Chapter Eleven: Key Takeaway Ideas

- ◆ In this chapter, we describe five key takeaway ideas to reflect on as you put the insights and examples described in this book into action in your classroom:

  - Reflect on and purposefully select technological tools.
  - Prioritize community building in remote instruction.
  - Emphasize collaboration and interaction.
  - Center students' ideas and experiences.
  - Be purposeful about communication and self-care.

We invite you to select one of those recommendations that especially stands out to you and reflect on how you'll incorporate it in your remote language arts instruction.

For Product Safety Concerns and Information please contact our
EU representative GPSR@taylorandfrancis.com Taylor & Francis
Verlag GmbH, Kaufingerstraße 24, 80331 München, Germany